RESILIENT
SPIRIT

Entrepreneurial Guiding Principles
& Leaps Of Faith That Create Success

RESILIENT SPIRIT
ENTREPRENEURIAL GUIDING PRINCIPLES
& LEAPS OF FAITH THAT CREATE SUCCESS

First edition. Feb. 1, 2025.

Published by Big Kat Kreative LLC, 2025.
Printed in the United States of America.

Cover designed by Michael Mazewski of Big Kat Kreative
Cover photo taken by Reagan Rule Photography

ISBN: 978-1-962796-07-1

Written by Sandy Stilwell Youngquist and Craig Handel.

RESILIENT SPIRIT

Entrepreneurial Guiding Principles
& Leaps Of Faith That Create Success

Sandy Stilwell Youngquist
With Craig Handel

To my family — a resilient force of nature,
as unwavering as the roots of the tallest tree.
Thanks for being there for me.

To the entrepreneurs among us, whose courage
to build dreams from scratch has shaped not
only our businesses but our legacies. For the times
we've celebrated our successes with pride and the
moments we've leaned on each other through losses,
proving that true wealth lies in our unity. Together,
we've weathered not just the storms of life, but the
hurricanes that reshaped the landscapes of our
homes and our hearts. Through shared stories,
emotional strength, and, at times, financial support,
we've become a testament to what determination
and hope can achieve. We are Resilient!

To the fearless, the hopeful, the unyielding — this
book is for you. Thank you for teaching me what
it means to endure, thrive and never give up.

This book is dedicated to God, who gives me
the strength to push forward and lean on
Him when my strength weakens.

Contents

Foreword 1
Introduction 11

PART 1: Pathways To Success

1: Young Entrepreneurs 19
2: Many Career Paths 27
3: New Technologies 37
4: Inspiring Women 47
5: Marketing, Goals
   And Making Money...................... 57
6: Borrowing Money 69
7: Balancing Faith, Family
   And Business 83

PART 2: The Sandy Side Of Business

8: From Windy City To Breezy Beaches   99
9: A Life Shaped At Age 10 111
10: Life By The Water 125
11: A Sister's Gift 133
12: Leadership 139
13: Running A Restaurant 149
14: Shared Vision 161
15: Uncommon Friends 167
16: Captiva's Charm 177
17: I Almost Bought An Island 187
18: Paying It Forward 197
19: Losing Great Minds 207

Sandy's Entrepreneurial Checklist ..   221
Acknowledgments 225
About The Authors 229

Foreword

Sandy Stilwell's energy and enthusiasm for her Southwest Florida community has impacted many lives, which is why it is appropriate to have two voices introduce her. Sandy's compassionate approach to business and her strong, faith-based leadership principles make her an inspiration to many.

Dr. Aysegul Timur, President, Florida Gulf Coast University
Sandy Stilwell Youngquist embodies what so many of our Florida Gulf Coast University students have become and will be – entrepreneurs, innovators and people who give back to their communities.

When my husband Mete and I came to Southwest Florida, people were so welcoming and warm we felt like adopted kids. I not only have great mentors but great friends. They are our chosen family.

Sandy, and her husband Tim, are among our chosen family. We have known each other for more than 20 years, going back to the days when I was a professor at Hodges University and Sandy was a trustee.

Sandy and I met at Hodges University when I was a professor

in 2007. She noticed my problem solving, enthusiasm and dedication when she was a member of the Board of Trustees. My starting an award-winning diversity program also caught her attention. She put in a good word with FGCU president Dr. Mike Martin, which helped in my hiring.

Sandy isn't just a strong, respected, female business leader, she is a thought leader. We have the same philosophy of going above and beyond and doing our best. And she always makes everything she touches look fabulous.

What also impresses me about Sandy is her commitment to higher education. I have listened to conversations where she has talked about investing in a work force as she believes that education is the best investment in human capital.

Her approach to lifelong learning also was exemplified by her education from Cornell University in Hospitality Management after establishing herself as an entrepreneur.

I truly believe in higher education but I understand it's not always a linear pathway. There are non-traditional or non-linear options of where and what you want to be.

Recognizing that many other Southwest Florida residents may be on a similar career path, FGCU has created digital badges that are micro-credentials, which can enhance one's resume by verifying to employers that individuals have the skills they want. The badges include three areas of focus to micro-credentials: industry-specific, transferable skills and continuing education and skills.

FGCU also has an adult-completion program so students do not have to take a traditional route to a university or be of a traditional age. Sandy is one of those non-traditional students and led by example to show to those around her what is possible if you never stop learning.

Meanwhile, FGCU's undergraduate entrepreneurship program – ranked No. 15 in The Princeton Review and

Entrepreneur magazine's top-50 undergraduate schools for Entrepreneurship Studies for 2023 – welcomes all students whether they are majors in the program or not.

Since 2016, students and alumni of the program have started over 374 businesses, raised $10.8 million in venture capital and earned more than $111 million in total gross revenue, according to director Sandra Kauanui. In the fall of 2023, there are 778 students in the undergraduate degree program – compared to 537 a year ago – with thousands more from other majors taking entrepreneurship classes.

If you're a history or music major and you have a business idea, we literally have open spaces – designed purposely – for students to come together and share entrepreneurial ideas and work as a group to discuss business plans.

For those of you interested in a tour, we have a maker's office on the second floor. In addition, many faculty members are entrepreneurship fellows.

FGCU also is connected with the community through the Small Business Development Center.

For young entrepreneurs looking for free education and advice in addition to financial assistance and loans, you can learn more by visiting this website: fsbdcswfl.org

FGCU's journey and my journey almost have run parallel.

In 1997, a need for a four-year institution was established in this region with the beginning of FGCU. The goal would not be about establishing a new workforce but sharing new, out-of-the box thinking. When we grow, the region grows. When the region grows, we grow.

In 1998, a young lady, with no English or language skills had the audacious goal of going to the best country in the world, the United States of America, and earning a PhD.

That was me, and I wanted to do it in economics. Where else to go but the best higher education in the world and the most capitalist nation?

FGCU has developed and established an innovative, entrepreneurial and technological spirit, which is shown in our water school, agribusiness program, school of entrepreneurship and other programs.

When I worked with senior professors as a teaching assistant, I worked in Microsoft Excel and PowerPoint. I told them, here's the next technology, you need to use it.

When I was a teaching assistant for students becoming masters in statistics, I also used Microsoft Excel. I told them you may need to do math on paper but you also need to learn this technology because it can help you make decisions.

I helped turn classrooms into being more experiential, more active, and ultimately, more popular.

And that's what I want FGCU to continue being: more cutting edge, more outside the box, more collaborative and more dynamic. I want FGCU to be an institution that Southwest Florida – and Sandy – always will be proud of as the university grows to support the community.

Wings Up and Go Eagles!

Gabriel Penton, Entrepreneur

Sometimes you have to ask a question.

Sometimes you have to take a risk.

That's what I did in high school and it has made a huge difference in my entrepreneurial journey.

On the last day of our Junior Achievement Class, Sandy Stilwell was leaving my classroom for the last time. I knew this was one of my first opportunities to connect with an actual entrepreneur. I took a leap and asked Sandy for a business card, taking her by surprise. However, upon closer review I realized it was missing an important component.

So I approached her.

"Is there any way you can give me your cell phone as well?" I asked.

She said yes.

After quickly writing it down and going off to other meetings while I went to Lunch B in the cafeteria of Cape Coral High School, I knew something important had taken place. Over time, thanks to my interactions with Sandy as well as her advice, I have learned so much about business. She has always been straightforward and doesn't sugarcoat her opinions. She's been battle-hardened in the realm of business in Southwest Florida, and many can say she's even revolutionized entrepreneurship with her ventures in Captiva in hospitality and food.

Thanks to her guidance and some doors she opened for me, I was able to connect with incredible entrepreneurs like Brian Rist, now a close friend and mentor. She also helped me push forward in school, speaking to the right people to let me take over six classes in a single semester.

I quickly realized her support was not an endorsement, but yet it provided an opportunity for me to push my limits and then realize there are other important factors in my life.

With Sandy, I enjoyed that she didn't give the fluff you find in most other entrepreneurs. A conversation with her will allow my analytical mind to see step-by-step what she did, and mimic it even if in a different venture.

I began doing real estate deals when I was 16, and many times I'd refer back to her journey. Entrepreneurship is most definitely not a linear regression. We spend years in the negative, or barely staying afloat only to one day grow exponentially, pinching ourselves in the morning about the life and company we've created.

Since I'm an analytical person, I wanted to dig deep about the keys to success in entrepreneurship and go beyond working hard. I got sick of that phrase.

Between ages 13 and 18, it's crazy how much I've been able to achieve. However, I recall my early stages with my first real business selling custom soaps in gift baskets to real estate agents, which led me to connect with incredible people, some of which I do business with on a much larger scale today. Needless to say, without Sandy advising me, and opening doors along the way, I may have made it to the same places but likely on a much longer trajectory.

While being the youngest student in the Entrepreneurship Program at Florida Gulf Coast University, I began assigning contracts for off-market properties in the Southwest Florida market to local and foreign investors. Since 2021, I have been involved in over a dozen fix-and-flip projects and 130 (and counting) land transactions. I've become the Director of Investments for a brokerage in Cape Coral and consulted with clients on a variety of projects.

What I've really enjoyed about entrepreneurship is the freedom I enjoy.

On a Thursday night, after six weeks of grueling Summer B courses, the night before my finals, I decided I wanted to go on a vacation – to Madrid. While my mom was expecting me to go back home and visit her in Orlando for the two-week gap until my final semester in the fall of 2024, I was determined to leave.

By then, I'd found a flight leaving that Friday at 9:35 p.m.

As a result of packing and handling my affairs before my departure, I made it an hour late to my finals yet still passed with flying colors. Then, I drove to Miami, and on the way there, I bought my ticket. Thirty minutes before boarding the plane – after checking into my flight – I'd gotten my hotel stay.

Having never been in Madrid before, and going on a one-way flight, I knew this would be an adventure. My social media feeds were blowing up from the surprise I had given everyone.

When asked how long I'd be gone, all I could answer was the truth – I don't know.

Being there, I convinced myself I was there for an adventure, not shopping or leisure, or sightseeing but rather a mixture of the three plus taking advantage of the nightlife offered by one of the cities that never sleeps.

However, on a walk down Calle Serrano, I found myself at a Golden Goose boutique staring at a pair of shoes that had been on my wish list, where most of my frivolous desires stay, a while. At first, I looked at it from an investment perspective realizing the shoes could be another week of vacation possibly, but then I also recognized all the sacrifice I'd made to get to where I was. Not just on the trip but in life.

I'd managed to get to my last semester of school debt-free, built a business, and created the life I'd envisioned for myself, but years earlier than I had planned. Much like Sandy, I had become successful at a young age, thanks to countless sacrifices. However, I also realized that there was much more to life than zeroes and ones.

I bought the shoes among other purchases, but I didn't regret it.

What's funny in this anecdote is that in the next 48 hours, I'd gotten more business whether by referrals, new opportunities, and previous clients without even looking for it. My phone would ring like crazy.

And even if I was in the middle of partying like most college students would dream of doing, I would always manage to pick up the phone.

Reflecting on not only my adventure but also my journey, I've realized the more that I got to know Sandy, the more that I learned about my own ambitions. I learned she made her first million early in life which was the first time I'd seen someone accomplish what I wanted. Every day the goal gets closer to being accomplished.

Thanks to Sandy's support and encouragement, I earned my bachelor's degree with a minor in real estate from FGCU at age 18. I was able to do this very quickly thanks to pulling a few strings, which mainly meant calling Sandy. I got approval. She told the professors, "If he can't handle it, he can drop a few courses."

I passed them all while excelling.

My next step is to go to law school somewhere in Florida. Sandy thinks I will get bored, but she agrees no one can defend your interests better than you. Using an entrepreneurial approach to law will allow me to look for solutions while managing risk, something most lawyers struggle with, simply because they aren't business-minded people.

I never liked to bother Sandy too much but every time we spoke, I learned something. Each conversation a gold nugget would enter my brain.

She taught me to:

> Find an industry I liked, learn that industry, find an opportunity and concentrate on a single niche, which becomes your forte. It's like the bread-and-butter theory.

> Be passionate about everyone and leave every business deal feeling, if possible, like you met a new friend.

Care for your employees, even when you suffer, like she did in the aftermath of Hurricane Ian. It reminded me of motivational speaker Zig Ziglar, who said, "You can get everything in life you want if you will help enough other people get what they want."

Envision the route in college that is right for me to become an entrepreneur. I did just that and graduated from college at 18. Other than taking a few courses, Sandy didn't go to college until later in life and she's just a well-rounded person who is wildly successful.

Enjoy the journey. I now aim to connect with people on a deeper level and develop a more keen insight of the world and how I fit in.

Sandy is involved in her foundation and charities as well as businesses. She's such a busy woman, but she always finds time because she cares about people. She believes in you and gives you opportunities to catapult yourself to the next level.

Two years after Sandy agreed to mentor me, I had the privilege of speaking at the Business Hall of Fame for Junior Achievement. It's a journey I never would've imagined had I not asked Sandy for her cell phone number. And it's a decision I don't regret.

Introduction:
The Best Is Yet To Be

"None of my inventions came by accident. I see a worthwhile need to be met and I make trial after trial until it comes. What it boils down to is one percent inspiration and 99 percent perspiration."

— Thomas Edison, *Uncommon Friends*

In the 1920s, a young man became friends with one of the greatest inventors of our time, Thomas Edison.

Though 50 years older, Edison and his wife Mina Miller welcomed the man in his 20s into their world. That meant he also shared the company of automobile pioneer Henry Ford, rubber magnate Harvey Firestone, aviator Charles Lindbergh and Alex Carrel, a French surgeon and biologist.

That man was James Newton. Using his relationships with the men above as the focus, he wrote a book called *Uncommon Friends*.

Among Jim's gems in the book was that Edison, who was

deaf for most of his life, taught Morse code to Mina, then used it to ask her to marry him.

In the 1970s, a young woman in her 20s became friends with Newton. Though 60 years older, he and wife Ellie welcomed this woman into their world. That meant she also met celebrities as well as top Southwest Florida entrepreneurs and political leaders.

That woman was me.

When he personally signed his book, Jim wrote:

For Sandy,

With gratitude for the great job you are doing for Uncommon Friends with your inspiration, creativity and commitment.

'The best is yet to be.'

Ellie says 'amen' to all of the above

Cheers
Jim Newton
4/18/96

Now I've written a book designed to be used as a teaching tool to encourage college students and young entrepreneurs. And yes, I'd like to continue the circle of helping to mentor people in their 20s and beyond.

I've also included life experiences and business advice from individuals I've worked and spent time with including entrepreneurs Deanna Wallin, Rachel Pierce, Brian Rist and Scott Fischer, husband Tim Youngquist, master marketers Colleen and Earl Quenzel, mental health activist

Dr. Alise Bartley and Dr. Aysegul Timur, the president at Florida Gulf Coast University.

While they all have wonderful stories, I wanted to have Dr. Timur write the foreword and share her inspirational story of going from a person who didn't speak English and being a teacher's aide to becoming the school's first woman and immigrant president.

Also writing a foreword is Gabriel Penton, a young man I mentored through Junior Achievement of Southwest Florida. Just 18, Gabriel already has graduated from FGCU with a business degree and has been part of the school's prestigious Daveler and Kauanui School of Entrepreneurship School.

Another member of that program, Jakub Adamowicz, shares his story and gives a shining example of the kind of talent coming out of Southwest Florida's young university.

Importance Of Mentoring

Studies have shown mentoring helps young people gain career and academic advice that sets them up for success when they enter the job market. It's also a way for students to explore various career options as they decide majors to pursue and industries to enter.

Mentoring also helps students put their goals on paper. Between 1979 and 1989, graduates of Harvard's MBA program were asked "Have you set clear written goals for your future and made plans to accomplish them?"

Only 3 percent had written goals and plans. However, that 3 percent has made 10 times as much as the other 97 percent combined.

The first seven chapters are on topics that young people face – what today's young entrepreneur looks like; varying paths to success; marketing; goal setting; women in the workplace; and borrowing money.

The second half of the book looks at experiences I've had – positive and negative.

I know of the mental health challenges many of you face – my family has gone through those – and I've had adversities many of you have dealt with. I don't want to keep score but the main thing I want to share is: How do we react when tough stuff comes our way?

I also share what a beautiful life you can have by working hard, connecting with the right business partners, choosing good mentors, and making good, honest decisions.

A lot of credit for my success goes to my God-directed life. I'm not shy about that. I'm not here to debate this point, I simply want to share what has worked for me.

I have conversations with God. I've even asked for the message to be so clear it must be written in the sky.

And God has sent signs, although I have not seen blue cursive in the white clouds.

God put wonderful people into my life; my incredible family and two others who came into my life in my 20s, Jim and Ellie Newton.

When we spoke, Jim focused on me and always wanted to know my opinion. For the first time, somebody wanted to know what I thought. I appreciated that. I also couldn't believe it. I was taught, "Speak when spoken to and respect your elders."

Ellie, often at Jim's side, also encouraged me to share my thoughts.

Jim prepared me for the naysayers.

"Some people will try to drive you down," he said. "Know who you are."

Know who you are. That just doesn't mean knowing your strengths but knowing your weaknesses. Leaders lead by focusing on their strengths. In areas where they're not as strong, they'll delegate and trust the people they hire. And when they make mistakes, they admit them.

Shortly after being interviewed for *Uncommon Friends of the Twentieth Century*, Jim died in 1999 at age 94. It was the same year I first invested in Captiva Island.

Jim never saw what I created and accomplished but he saw me as I grew into who I am. He was right. The best was yet to be.

Jim always said mentorship is about aligning yourself with others so they're helping you as much as you're helping them.

On the pages that follow, I'll share my entrepreneurial path, my parental influences and good and bad life lessons. I'll also highlight the friends and mentors that have helped me on my journey.

I've structured this book with questions after every chapter because I'm interested in you.

I'm interested in your background.

I'm interested in your goals.

I'm interested in your ideas.

I'm interested in your way of thinking.

And I'm interested in your answers to the questions you'll need to ask yourself to become a successful entrepreneur.

A mentor showed the same interest in me and it made all the difference in the world.

PART 1:
Pathways To Success

CHAPTER 1

Young Entrepreneurs

---

*"If you aim at nothing,
you will hit it every time."*

– Zig Ziglar

Being an entrepreneur is incredibly fulfilling.

Working with young entrepreneurs is incredibly rewarding.

Brian Rist, the former owner of Storm Smart, and I thoroughly enjoy interacting with young people.

"Teaching is one of the most fun things I've done," Brian said. "Watching their eyes light up as you share your experiences is an incredible high.

"It's a unique position. You're in a situation where you surround yourself with kids who are trying to make themselves better. In the workforce, you often run into people who are happy where they're at.

"Now, you have to be on your toes. They'll challenge you. You gotta be prepared and think through things."

I love working with young people. They are interested, curious and eager to learn. As parents, we do our best to teach and instill values in our children, but oftentimes those lessons truly sink in when they are reinforced by a third party.

Many times it's them hearing the same things from me, but they appreciate it coming from somebody other than their parents. Students are brilliant, and they want to explore other opinions.

When speaking with a large group of students, I'll always have a few who are just not engaged in the conversation. There will be others who are moderately involved, but the bright and shining students rise to the top, as they are truly engaged in the class and conversation.

I focus on the truly engaged students, and this often leads those moderately interested to become more fully engaged. Those who are there only to fulfill requirements will get exactly what they put into each class.

Over the years, my interactions with young people have led to me employing some of them, recommending them for

With Gabriel Penton, pictured left, and Brian Rist at the Junior Achievement Awards, where Gabriel spoke about the entrepreneurial class and how we met.

jobs elsewhere, or just being a resource for them if they need a recommendation or advice.

Occasionally, we work with young entrepreneurs who already are armed with significant experience.

Gabe Penton, highlighted in the foreword, and Jakub Adamowicz, another young business owner, are proof that business success can happen at any age.

Like Gabe, Jakub didn't inherit an empire from his parents. They both learned how to work hard.

But they also learned about creating their own niche. They worked with professors at the Daveler and Kauanui School of Entrepreneurship School at Florida Gulf Coast University, they took constructive criticism, they asked good questions and they built their brands.

Some aspects of Jakub's journey are what we'll see from future entrepreneurs, particularly when it comes to using technology. He also was motivated to take a different path from his parents' fix-and-flip business when he found himself caked in concrete on a hot day in New York City.

"I remember saying, 'I don't care how hard I have to work but I want to be in an air-conditioned office sipping coffee while being in front of a computer,' " Jakub recalled.

As a youth, he started playing the video game *Minecraft*, which came out in 2011. Called a 'sandbox' game because there are a lot of ways it can be played, creative uses can shape the blocks and build a variety of objects based on one's imagination. Blocks can be broken, crafted and placed to reshape the landscape. Or they can be used to build fantastical creations.

While moving on to Microsoft Gaming's Xbox platform and the military science fiction franchise *Halo*, Jakub kept learning more about software. He soon was paid by making spoof websites. He made even more money by creating a server on his computer. It also allowed him to play video games with more than just one friend.

"I had an idea to put the server on a cloud before a cloud server ever was a thing," Jakub recalled. "Because the room was overheating, we'd open the window in the winter. In the summer, air conditioning cost us so much money that my parents wanted me to shut it down.

"If I had kept that server running, I'd probably be a billionaire now."

By building a metaverse and worlds with these video games, Jakub started selling subscriptions for $15 a month. That may not sound like much until thousands of users around the world bought subscriptions.

After Jakub became one of the world's top *Halo* players by working his way to the highest levels, he then sold those programs while offering his services as a trainer. If you're counting at home, that's three different income streams.

"I had started a business without even knowing it," he said "It was fun. When I opened a bank account, I had no clue you had to link PayPal with a bank account."

As a teen, Jakub bought a BMW with cash. The car salesman thought his mother was buying the vehicle.

When the money kept flowing in, Jakub helped his parents – whose company struggled during the Wall Street crash – pay their mortgage.

A talented basketball player who traveled in the highly competitive Amateur Athletic Union (AAU) circuit – the 6-foot-3 Jakub was invited to a camp at the University of Duke, one of the top college basketball teams in the country. It was there he met his future wife, Sarah.

He strongly considered attending Holy Cross but injuries and his future wife's charms led him to Florida Gulf Coast University.

Forgoing basketball and focusing on a degree in engineering, Jakub started his first company, *Room Dig*, an online platform to help college students find housing and roommates, now available for use at universities across the country.

Think of Match.com for roommates. The business won him statewide recognition in Florida and designation as a 2018 Forbes 30 Under 30 Fellow.

He didn't stop there. About the same time Jakub established *Room Dig*, he had an idea about transforming the real estate business, whose main structures had changed little since 1908.

Before he graduated in 2022 with a master's in entrepreneurship at FGCU, he said he's been part of $100 million in real estate transactions since he got involved in the business at 18.

Jakub Adamowicz is a bright young mind who sees problems and creates solutions, which is the approach all entrepreneurs need.

When talking about real estate in the last 115-plus years, Jakub said, "They didn't have Apple and cell phones and DocuSign back then.

"We have all these technologies, and you can sell a home using 10 different tools. I'm thinking, 'Hey, why not be the one who combines all these different tools into one site?' "

Jakub named his company *Listella*. He feels what separates

Listella from other realtors and real-estate companies is that the company is independent of the buyer or seller. The other differences are the appraisal and inspection are done before the listing.

He also takes a fraction of the 6 percent commissions many other realtors charge.

"I can understand real-estate agents hand-holding billionaires who want gold-handled doors and gold toilets," he said. "But what about deployed veterans or workers who must change locations regularly?"

Taking that competitive nature from gaming, playing basketball and building servers, Jakub wants *Listella* to top Zillow as the No. 1 place where people go to buy and sell homes.

But he feels he has another side. He feels like a lot of people in his generation who would like to make a difference in the world and help others. "I've always felt I was put on earth to make an impact greater than myself," he said. "Our younger generation wants to help the environment, animals and the economic system."

There's some old school in him. Even though basketball was a passion, he didn't study Michael Jordan as much as Andrew Carnegie.

"I like to work on the complicated but (entrepreneurship) doesn't have to be complicated," he said. "There's young entrepreneurs making millions by making slime."

Or selling cold brews.

Or selling equine supplements.

Or having an online estate agency.

Or monetizing how to start a business.

Yes business ideas abound among young entrepreneurs. Through FGCU's Small Business Development Center, Suzanne Specht – a former loan officer – has consulted with approximately 3,000 small business owners. That has ranged from business plans to financial statements to loan applications resulting in more than 200 business start-ups and capital formation of more than $50 million dollars. Specifically, Suzanne facilitated the State of Florida Bridge Loan program for the Southwest Florida area during Hurricane Irma.

That's just one university institution.

But there are a number of ways of educating yourself to become an entrepreneur and begin to build businesses.

Entrepreneurial Mindset Q&A:

———————

When you think of the word entrepreneur, what does that mean to you?

When you had your first job, did that inspire you to work in that field?

When you had your first job, did that motivate you to stay in that field or to find your own niche?

What business idea do you have?

Who have you approached about your business idea?

What are your goals and dreams professionally?

CHAPTER 2

Many Career Paths

"I teach at a university and I'm pro university;
but I think it's a terrible mistake in high school
to push a youth into a box that is college."

– Former Storm Smart owner Brian Rist,
a professor at Florida Gulf Coast University

Scott Fischer always has enjoyed motorcycles.

He liked putting them together, even though that required him to assemble hundreds of pieces.

He enjoyed racing them.

He also enjoyed working around the machines, even if it meant his first job was sweeping floors.

"I couldn't wait to go to a motorcycle store to see what I could do," he said.

He – and his parents – didn't consider secondary education.

"I didn't grow up in a family that was focused on college," he said. "It wasn't a discussion. My real focus in growing was I had to work. If I wanted to have the things I wanted to have, I had to work for it."

Scott worked his way up – quickly – to become a Harley Davidson dealership owner at the age of 27. At their peak in 2014, Scott Fischer Enterprises had $121 million in annual revenue and some 360 employees spread through dealerships in Alabama, North Carolina, New Mexico and California as well as Southwest Florida. Two successful dealerships in New Mexico remain in his name.

Traditional thinking has been to go to college and get a four-year degree and then a master's degree, maybe a doctorate. That mindset is changing and especially for entrepreneurs.

My path, and my husband Tim Youngquist's path, resembled Scott's.

Scott Fischer has proven that when you combine your passion with hard work, it can be the foundation of an amazing career.

Instead of a four-year school, I started a couple of businesses, bought a home and took a few non-accredited courses in the evenings at Edison State College.

An avid reader, I read books professors recommended.

After buying three businesses and eight properties, I returned to school where I attended Cornell's Hospitality Management School at age 40.

Just within my own family, there are many examples of unique pathways to successful careers.

Tim Youngquist and his brother Harvey went to work immediately after high school and found their niche in doing small wells and irrigation. They started a company called Youngquist Brothers. As they made profits, they started buying, developing and drilling land. Their travels took them to Houston, Oklahoma City, North Dakota and Montana as well as Southwest Florida.

"We didn't start with much," Tim said. "We didn't have any money. We just continued to do what we started to do and got better at it. Now, we're the largest drillers in the state."

Their businesses expanded into rock mining, oil and gas field services, water quality testing and dating analysis, in-house equipment fabrication and contract manufacturing, general contracting and medical device manufacturing.

While Tim thinks college and trade schools are good, he agrees with Brian Rist that going to a university isn't for everyone.

"Don't waste four, five years in college if you don't think college will do you any good," he said. "When people come here and go to work early, they become a powerhouse. The family can teach you about engineering and business. You're not wasting your time.

"You're young and you can train and work hard in those early years."

Youngquist family members who joined the business have become powerhouses. Those who have gone to college have returned and complemented the operations at Youngquist Brothers.

The family-owned Bayfront Inn was run by Tim's daughter, Trista Kragh. They sold it at the perfect time after Hurricane Ian. It didn't sustain much damage, and it housed many construction workers after the hurricane.

Her husband Matthew owns MHK Architecture & Planning. He started off in Naples, Florida, and has now expanded to offices all over the United States, including

As an entrepreneur, you'll work hard to earn your success, but it's equally important to relax, too. On a getaway to New York City, my husband Tim and I had this photo taken with the Statue of Liberty.

Palm Beach, Islamorada in the Florida Keys, Sarasota and Sanibel Island in Florida; Charleston and Greenville in South Carolina; Highlands, North Carolina; and Denver. They provide drawings and designs for many *Youngquist Brothers* projects.

They try their best to keep it all in the family.

Three of Harvey's children also have joined the team.

Harvey Youngquist, Jr. is an engineer for the local well-drilling operation while Holly Youngquist Herbers is a licensed realtor who worked with her father and uncle while leasing out their Gulfcoast Industrial Campus. Brett Youngquist manages and operates Texas Home Development near Houston and development projects in Florida. They are about to expand further.

Their other daughter, Brooke Sweat, competed in the 2016

Summer Olympics in beach volleyball and is a graduate of FGCU. She still is competing and enjoys mentoring young athletes.

The Cost Of College

With the rising costs of colleges – many exceeding the rise in inflation – young entrepreneurs are opting for practical experience over an undergraduate degree.

Since 2020, enrollment into universities has dropped.

The COVID-19 worldwide pandemic, which led to many people reevaluating their lives, played a factor in this trend.

When it came time for students to return to their campuses in 2021, fewer showed up than during the worst months of the pandemic in the fall of 2020.

The number of undergraduate students dropped by about 3 percent in the 2021-22 academic year after plunging 3.4 percent during the 2020-21 pandemic year, according to preliminary data released by the National Student Clearinghouse Research Center. That equaled about 6.5 percent fewer undergraduate students than in the fall of 2019 before the pandemic.

Highly successful entrepreneurs also have noticed something anecdotally.

Robert Kiyosaki said there is an inverse relationship developing between advanced degrees and getting rich. He also noticed that 'A' students often end up working for 'C' students.

And that's often because Kiyosaki noted 'C' students tend to be more educated on life skills best learned through experience rather than the classroom.

He feels we've gone from an industrial age to an informational age and schools haven't caught up.

In Sidney Simon's book *Wad-Ja-Get? The Grading Game in American Education*, the former university professor said students should be much more concerned with what they learned as opposed to what grade they received.

However, depending on your path, you need to determine the best route for yourself.

Traditional Route

Brian Rist has gone full circle from student to professor and mentor. In between, his innovations led to a highly profitable business.

After learning about the garment, dry-cleaning and coin-operated laundry businesses from his parents, he earned a degree in Operations Management from the University of Massachusetts Lowell.

An innovator in home protection against hurricanes, Rist started Storm Smart in 1996 and built it into a $50 million business with 250 employees. In 2021, he sold controlling interest in the company to Rotunda Capital Partners, a lower-middle market private equity firm. Rist retained a significant equity interest in the company.

"I thought if you take care of customers, the business will take care of you," Rist said. "Then I realized, if you take care of your employees, they'll take care of your customers and then they'll help take care of you.

"We found 62 percent of our business was referral-based. Mother, brother, sister, cousin."

Before he sold his company, Rist went back to school at UMass Lowell as an online student in the Master of Business Administration program. The course he took: Managing Organizational Change.

"You have to change," Rist said. "If you stay the way you are, you become a dinosaur. You gotta keep going and get ahead of things."

After he sold his company, Rist gifted both FGCU and

UMass Lowell, then became a professor and mentor for students at those institutions.

"I'm fortunate because most of the students kind of know my story," he said. "I'm from the business world, which is a tremendous advantage for people like Scott and Sandy when they teach.

"When you tell them there are good days and bad days, their eyes light up. There will be dark days. Many businesses fail. But I learned that businesses don't fail, people quit. I didn't quit."

Common Denominator

While he went the traditional route and earned a bachelor's and master's, Rist said "There's a thousand ways to learn" while totally backing those interested in going into trade school.

"I teach at a university and I'm pro university but I think it's a terrible mistake in high school to push someone into a box that is college," he said. "Those who have gone into the trades or gotten certified or even the military are often so much further ahead.

"We work with the community and we've taken a lot of kids out of high school and they've done well. One of the reasons we're so involved with FSW (Florida Southwestern College) is that 78 percent of the graduates are debt-free."

Conversely, Scott Fischer believed in learning as much as he could at an early age. Shortly after he became a business owner, he paid to implement training, coaching and systems for his employees, some of whom have become owners and general managers in other companies.

"In my young career, I was focused on being a student of the business," he said. "Even though I didn't go to college, there are key elements of education. There are programs in our industry. We were sharing information, the whole purpose of what's happening in our business and learning from peers. I surrounded myself with professionals – advisors, an attorney, key people you have to have. I had them, not just because I needed them but because I wanted them to help me understand that part of the business.

"When you associate yourself with those kinds of people, you understand you're not the smartest guy. Once you quit talking, you can learn a lot when you listen."

What Are Your Strengths?
I applaud someone who receives honors while earning a college degree, but I also appreciate someone who gets certified in a specialty from a trade school or took a path similar to me.

There are many ways to succeed. One way is no better than another. There are book learners, there are practical learners and there are active learners. The key is to understand the environment you excel in.

Book learning: Books can put you in your own world where authors share thoughts and ideas that increase the reader's sense of perspective. In the meantime, the readers' own thoughts and ideas are stimulated. But no matter whether the book learning is done in school or on one's own, it needs to be done to expand knowledge.

Practical learning: Also called experiential learning, it is learning through doing hands-on things such as experimentation in laboratories or study tours.

Active learning: It's a classroom approach that focuses on how the students learn, not just what they learn.

For me, I like the literal meaning of learning as you do it. Putting up a curtain while learning how to design a home. Doing your own accounting while managing payroll.

Entrepreneurs are multi-taskers. We are the repair and maintenance department, we are the human resource decision makers, the buyer, the seller and the complaint department. The saying that the buck stops here is very true.

This brings us to internships.

There are hotels like Marriott and Hyatt where a person can start at the front desk, then work in food and beverage, sales, reservations and upper- end housekeeping and maintenance.

Same with restaurants – busboy, waiter or waitress, host, short-order cook and restaurant manager.

In both cases, you are paid while learning.

No job is too low. Like Scott and Brian, there are successful people I know who started as dishwashers, mowed lawns, babysat children and sold sandwiches out of their uncle's yogurt shop.

All experience is valuable.

One of the most important things to understand about the hospitality industry is the work hours, particularly when you're young.

There's a lot of late nights, weekends and holidays with most of those jobs. When you start to raise a family, that becomes a big consideration. The incentive to avoid those hours is working hard, having a good mentor and learning how to get into management.

Entrepreneurial Mindset Q&A:

Would you rather go to a university, junior college, trade school or get certified?

Are you happy with what you are doing now? If not, what would you like to do?

Is there anything you want to change about your career path?

What is stopping you from doing so?

Are you more interested in getting good grades or applying what you learn into the workforce?

Do you want to make a lot of money? Do you want a job that stirs your passions? Or do you want a job that is an asset to your community?

CHAPTER 3

New Technologies

"We're taking old practices and leveraging what technology we can use."

— Earl Quenzel, marketing expert and co-owner of Quenzel & Associates

---

Artificial Intelligence (AI), Search Engine Optimization (SEO), pay-per-click (PPC), apps, iPads, iPhones, Kindles, social media, Zoom calls, QR codes and digital billboards are some of the growing numbers of technologies at our fingertips.

Television channels have gone from ABC, CBS, NBC and PBS to dozens and now hundreds. TV streaming services compete with cable companies.

Satellite radio has exploded with hundreds of channels, fragmenting the airwaves.

Websites used to be hard-coded by programmers. Now there are platforms like WordPress that make building websites less daunting.

The new technologies not only have their own languages, but they've made our lives easier, more convenient, and in many ways, less costly. But is it better?

I have mixed emotions as do other entrepreneurs.

It's not that we're established business owners and set in our ways. We do see the value. We have harnessed these emerging technologies for our businesses.

But is it making life too easy? Are we thinking enough? Also, are we relying too much on technology and not enough on the human element? Are we succumbing to the machines?

Here are a few pros and cons of innovation.

Technology Pros

Technology has made our world smaller.

We can communicate with – and see – family, friends and business associates through What's Ap, Facebook's Messenger, Zoom calls and FaceTime from all over the world. That has led to people connecting more and spending less time driving and flying.

Less use of paper records, phone books, newspapers, magazines and books has saved millions of trees.

Bills can be paid without using postage. QR codes have replaced coupons. Food can be delivered to your home. Comparison shopping can be done easily on devices, saving people money on groceries, home furnishings and everyday household items.

Technology also has led to freedom of expression. Even better, it has raised awareness of social causes or personal hardships. GoFundMe accounts have greatly helped those in need.

Savvy use of social media can save thousands in advertising for those starting businesses. People who can deliver messages in 140 characters or less, write compelling copy on Facebook, or take enticing photos on Instagram cannot only be successful entrepreneurs, but maybe even successful influencers, an emerging profession that can be a lucrative career path.

A thorough understanding of pay-per-click advertising, such as search engine advertising or Google Ads, can also reduce costs by reaching your target audience in a particular area or connecting with customers in-market for your products or services.

It's good to stay curious and be open-minded with new technologies, which is why I experimented with Artificial Intelligence to fine-tune the marketing and business plan that I created.

I did it my old-fashioned way first, as I created an outline and then filled in the blanks to complete my Business Plan. I always use this framework for my outline:

Business Plan:
- Executive Summary
- Company Description
- Market Analysis
- Organization and Management
- Product or Services
- Marketing and Sales Strategy
- Operational Plan
- Financial Plan
- Funding Needs
- Additional helpful information includes my bio or resume, legal documentation, permits and any applicable information.

It took about a week's time to gather the information and get it all together in what I felt was a very good presentation.

Then I went to AI and asked it to create a business plan for X. In this case it wasn't a restaurant. It was a resort. I used all of the keywords to describe what and where the business would be. It can only do what you give clear directions for it to do.

Once I finished feeding in the data, it only took about 60 seconds for it to output a business plan that almost mirrored my plan, but it was much more eloquent in the descriptions. I was then able to edit my version into a better version, though I still needed to put some sweat equity into it.

After that, I worked on my Marketing Plan. I had a budget and allocated a certain amount toward each line item.

I drilled down a bit for the marketing plan. To have a multichannel strategy, we must allocate a certain amount to internet-based advertising, print ads, radio, TV, sponsorships, etc.

It took about a week to complete the project. I found the time saver was in the marketing plan because I asked AI to adjust my allocation percentages for advertising to the national standard in tourism by dividing the marketing budget. Again, it came back in 60 seconds with a budget. It made me feel excellent because it closely mirrored what I came up with.

The AI version was much more polished, and I was able to adjust my marketing plan accordingly. I'm not a proponent of relying on AI to do our work. You know the old saying, "garbage in equals garbage out."

You need to know your product to spot an inaccuracy. Yet, AI helps me with spreadsheets and projections. Should I buy a piece of equipment, or should I lease it? If it's a lease with free maintenance, you can calculate it based upon past costs in repairing a similar item. Should I buy my ice machine or should I lease it? Once you've been in business a while, you'll find that keeping very accurate records will help you save money down the line.

What surprised me was how fast AI spit out the information. It was almost scary.

Technology readily makes data available. The biggest challenge is translating that data into ways to attract more customers.

When opening a new business, I've found it extremely helpful to hire a marketing firm. One example of how pivotal this support can be happened when I was re-opening an existing restaurant. This group did a full Market Analysis for me.

What they determined in a week saved me lots of money during the time that I owned the business. The research helped me change the name of the restaurant because it did not clearly describe what kind of restaurant it was. We clarified the name and changed the logo.

Colleen and Earl Quenzel helped me with that. After working for a variety of businesses and marketing-related companies, they settled in Southwest Florida in 2005 where they own Quenzel & Associates.

"We get reports that have 40 pages of data," Colleen Quenzel said. "We go to cause and effect and continue to the bottom line.

"Before, there were three or four options so you knew you could cut the pie in four pieces. Now, it's cut into 100s of pieces."

Technology Cons

For as much good as technology has done, there are many ways it has been used for bad, even evil.

All you need to know are three words – The Dark Web.

Not far behind are hackers.

Data breaches have led to billions of records being stolen every year, ruining businesses. They're a new form of espionage. While they can be a national security threat, 86 percent are about money, and 55 percent are committed by organized criminal groups, according to Verizon's annual data breach report.

Personally, there have been a lot of problems with the addictive nature of social media for some people, particularly the young.

As actress Mae West once said, "Too much of a good thing is too much."

The amount of screen time is alarming. So are people turning social media into popularity contests where those not faring as well in the likes, comments and retweets are belittled.

And then there are the stories of those whose political views or comments were so severe that it led to people losing their jobs, losing credibility and even being arrested.

"Kids need to be careful about what they post," FGCU professor and former Storm Smart owner Brian Rist said. "That is dangerous. They never know how long something they post will follow them. Also be careful what is said about employers."

As I mentioned, I liked AI for its ability to dispense information in quantity and speed. However, I noticed that the information was generic and not that detailed.

I also don't like how much misinformation or disinformation can be posted as fact, when in fact, it is not.

There are the podcasters out there that gather a following and get paid by sensationalism. People's reputations can be harmed when things are reported like the truth and it's hard to get it taken off of the web.

Many people write and get paid based on how many times their stories are viewed, clicked on or shared. There seems to be no real accountability, and one questions whether they care.

Libel is written defamation, and slander is spoken defamation. Both are supposed to be illegal in the United States, and defamation can lead to criminal sanctions. However, libel and slander only exist in a handful of states and are rarely enforced.

When laws aren't enforced, abuse can cross the line and the end result often leads to either bullying, ruining reputations or causing long-lasting harm. There are laws passed to protect, but there is much more to do to protect people from this sort of abuse.

Fortunately, in Florida they have really cracked down on this. Our Attorney General and the entire team of decision makers took this very seriously. We are allowed to protect ourselves, but we have to hire attorneys to help. So always be careful what you write or say about somebody. It's their reputation, but it's yours as well. I have found it the best policy to follow my mother's advice: If you can't say something positive about somebody, then it's probably better not to say anything at all.

Of course, there are exceptions. But, it's a good rule of thumb. Also, I never speak disparagingly about any competitor's business. Only talk about what you can do, what your company can do. Don't worry about the competition. Just do your very best job to the best of your ability and stay focused on your goal.

Free speech – one key area separating the United States from government-run countries – has become the Wild West. This has to be monitored carefully.

From a business standpoint, something that is supposed to be a positive – reviews – can be a negative if there are nasty competitors or people who just don't like you.

Five-star reviews are great, Colleen Quenzel said, but if there are too many, customers may think your product is too perfect. She added sometimes the best review is if a customer brings up a problem and the business owner addresses it in a timely fashion.

Conversely, reviews can be manipulated by a person or persons who want to see your business fail. Reviews, like the quality of your food, have to be monitored.

There is a sad but true fact – not everybody is happy for your success.

One of my big issues with technology is that we've made it too easy for our children. There seems to be less problem-solving, less thinking and less collaboration. Too much of the critical thinking and connecting is being done artificially.

I am concerned that when faced with adversity, many young people often have difficulty handling it.

Also, is technology taking time away from young people that they might otherwise spend on exercise, meditation, quiet time or meeting up with friends? I wonder.

And that leads me to a final point.

Human Connection

Brian Rist believes digital communication has its place, but he doesn't know if young entrepreneurs understand the quality of social networking.

"If you need a job, loan or customers, that's the way to get things done," he said. "You have to get out, meet other people and talk.

"You may not be comfortable at first but by doing it hundreds of times, you get better at talking to people."

That's why Brian supports FGCU's Runway program because students must pitch ideas and concepts. Verbally.

As Brian said earlier, 62 percent of his Storm Smart business came from referrals.

Colleen Quenzel said businesses thrive by word of mouth,

especially in this day and time. However, she said close to 90 percent don't know what their ideal customer is and how to reach them.

Colleen and Earl said some of their best data comes from customer or patient research.

The Quenzels had one Sanibel market owner who was convinced that most families shopped for their groceries before arriving at their condos. The Quenzels' research showed that they would unpack, get situated in their condos, then go shopping.

"Research showed that going out shopping and choosing the meal was a highlight for the kids as well as the parents," Earl Quenzel said. "Many people would arrive on Saturday afternoons when the condos changed. So we ran ads Saturday night, Sunday morning and Sunday night and then we'd stop.

"We drove at least one visit. For those people who knew an alternative market, instead of finding his market on the fourth visit, they found it on the second or third. It was a difference of 15 to 20 percent in revenue."

A detailed 20-minute questionnaire for customers can reveal plenty.

"I've had business owners tell me that customers won't take 20 minutes to do that," Colleen Quenzel said. "I said your best customers will take the time. They may bring up something that's important to know."

I have always relished personal contact with customers, other entrepreneurs, and even competitors. I'm a believer that there is enough business to go around and that by being a connector, that positive vibe, that positive karma, may just come back to me.

And it's just the right thing to do.

Entrepreneurial Mindset Q&A:

What do you like best about technology?

Is there any part of technology you don't like?

Do you rely on technology too much?

Are you concerned that technology has led to less human thinking and problem-solving?

How do you think you would integrate technology into your business?

CHAPTER 4

Inspiring Women

"I am woman, hear me roar
In numbers too big to ignore
And I know too much to go back an' pretend
'cause I've heard it all before
And I've been down there on the floor
No one's ever gonna keep me down again

Oh yes I am wise
But it's wisdom born of pain
Yes, I've paid the price
But look how much I gained
If I have to, I can do anything
I am strong (strong)
I am invincible (invincible)
I am woman"

- Helen Reddy, "I Am Woman"

Deanna Wallin and Rachel Pierce became entrepreneurs a bit later in their lives but through ingenuity, connections, problem solving and hard work, they have built highly successful businesses.

Deanna, who was a nurse before going into medical sales, started Naples Soap Company born from her own health challenges. She has built that business to 13 locations in Florida.

Rachel, who worked in television for 19 years, started donating her works of art at various Southwest Florida galas and charity events. People then either commissioned her to create custom paintings or bought her pieces. She now has two art galleries, a furniture and accessories store and a boutique pet store.

It's a great time to be a woman entering the workforce. In fact, it may be the best time in our country's history.

Statistics show that:

- For the first time in the 68-year history of the Fortune 500 lists, women are leading more than 10 percent of Fortune 500 companies. On Jan. 1, 2023, start dates of five new Fortune 500 chief executives brought the number of female CEOs up to 53, pushing the tally over the long-awaited threshold. So, the percentage is closer to 11 percent.

- In 2020, women made up 47 percent of new business owners, a significant jump from 29 percent in 2019, according to a report from Gusto, which operates a payroll, benefits and HR platform.

- The labor force participation rate for women in their prime working age hit an all-time high in June of 2023, reaching 77.8 percent, according to the Bureau of Labor Statistics.

- Young women are more likely to be enrolled in college today than young men. Among those ages 25 and older, women are more likely than men to have a four-year college degree. The gap in college completion is even wider among younger adults ages 25 to 34. This comes from the Pew Research Group.

Deanna Wallin's Success Story

As she watches young entrepreneurs start health and wellness brands, Deanna Wallin watches approvingly, but also maybe a bit enviously.

"They put a lot of effort in and have been given a lot of attention," Deanna said. "It's refreshing. I can tell you it wasn't there (in 2009).

"They still call me a young entrepreneur. No, no, no. I'm old now. I'm a pioneer."

There's a lot to be envious about Deanna's business – Naples Soap Company – which made $12.5 million in revenue in those 13 locations. "One in 25 businesses ever top $10 million," she said.

While she's made money, Deanna has had a hard time borrowing and raising capital. From 2009 until now, she's found it to be a constant tug-of-war.

"In the beginning, in my industry, the personal care and beauty industry was very challenging to get financing and banking to take us seriously," she said. "That was just so frustrating then and still is today.

"The traditional, male-run business banking, financing and investment funds were condescending. COVID changed a lot of that, and diversity, equity and inclusion led to a movement."

Deanna considered private equity companies but didn't

like that they wanted too much control – especially since they didn't strike her as having a strong knowledge of her industry.

"That's why we try to find the right partners," she said. "The wrong people can lead you down a path you don't want to go. We experienced that. People that come in act as if they know how to run our business better than we do. Maybe they didn't understand how a product needed to be promoted? I am my own consumer, and I know what I want to buy."

A nurse for eight years, Deanna had been bothered by eczema and psoriasis. In a transition phase of her life, she had a friend visit and notice how many soaps and lotions she had.

Ingenuity helped Deanna Wallin create a better natural soap and led her to transition from nurse to thriving entrepreneur.

When the friend asked why, Deanna said, "I have eczema. This works, this doesn't, and this did work but no longer does. When I said I like natural soaps the best, he said, 'Sell what you know.' "

Because of her wide-ranging knowledge as a nurse having worked in pediatrics and geriatrics, she had a good idea what ingredients she wanted in her products while she could offer a wide range of advice.

"When someone asks us what our demographics are, we say babies to 80s," Deanna said. "At the start, we opened a 300-square-foot store, which is about closet size, and we started adding products. People came in and talked about skin issues. They came from 50 to 60 miles away. Within four months, we tore our wall down and expanded."

As she added locations and saw people buy her online products from all over the country, Deanna has persevered through five major events – four hurricanes and a global pandemic.

"In 2017, Hurricane Irma ripped off the roof in my store in Tin City," she said. "A few months later my father died, and I also had a divorce, which lasted three years. I also have seen employees lose their homes and sleep in our office while in tears. I dealt with COVID when the world shut down."

"What I say is, 'Where there's a will, there's a way. We were constant problem solvers. We did something that hadn't been done or did it in a different way. I figure I'm a crisis management expert. You stay positive and calm but you're working on adrenaline."

Naples Soap Company Wholesale division distributes products to 300 boutiques, spas and stores throughout the United States.

In 2024, Florida's Small Business Development Center at Florida Gulf Coast University awarded Deanna the Distinguished Entrepreneur Award. That marked her eighth honor recognizing her leadership, business acumen and entrepreneurial talent from numerous organizations.

Even with success comes issues. Every time Naples Soap Company reached a milestone in revenue earnings, she hit growth hurdles.

Expansion. More inventory. Increasing lines of credit. Managing growth. Buying less expensive products internationally. Payroll. Trim fat. Discard services that her company outgrew.

Lots of challenges but it beats the alternative.

Deanna tells young entrepreneurs, "If you have the vision and passion, stay true to it. Surround yourself with smart yet supportive people who won't alter your vision. And don't get derailed."

Rachel Pierce's Success Story

Growing up in Chippewa Falls, Wisconsin – where five fictional characters lived, including Annie Hall – Rachel Pierce remembers going with her creative mom, Jenny Licht, to art shows in the Dakotas and Ozarks.

"We'd get up in the middle of the night and drive eight hours or more," she said. "We'd set up and be ready to start at 10 a.m. on Saturdays. I'd do face paintings and I had my sandwich-board stand. I'd charge one dollar. I paid for my first car a dollar at a time."

Rachel Pierce is a great example of following your heart and working hard to find success, even if it means changing careers.

Even as she went to college in Oklahoma City and then worked in TV markets in Eau Claire, Wisconsin; Omaha, Nebraska; and Des Moines, Iowa; before landing in Fort Myers, Florida, she still painted for family and friends.

"I painted a platter for Ronald McDonald House which led people to say, 'Oh my gosh, you're really good.' It kept snowballing, but I just did it to donate.

"At one point, Lisa O'Neill wanted me to paint a painting.

I wondered, 'Is it legal to make money outside my job?' "

Taking the approach of asking for forgiveness later rather than seeking to get permission, Rachel started to have people commission her work like me. On my yacht, she painted a sea turtle.

"Sea turtles, they're kind of my jam," she said. "Sandy kept giving me opportunities while I was still on TV. She then introduced me to her circle of friends. She's always been good at mentoring."

In July 2019, Rachel had her fourth child, Daphne, joining Rory, Piper and Lydia. With COVID-19 making her TV job harder but her art job easier, Rachel followed through on her thoughts of getting out of television. When her contract was up a year later, she didn't renew it.

Rachel hit the ground with her feet running when she left NBC2 in Fort Myers on June 26, 2020.

The ladies I look up to and who are my friends. Choose your friends wisely. Pictured from left to right: former CEO Sarah Owen, FGCU President Aysegul Timur, me, Senator Lizbeth Benacquisto and business pioneer Gail Markham Meurer.

She opened art galleries on Sanibel Island and at the Bell Tower Shops in Fort Myers in 2022, then a home furnishings store and Paw Paradise after Island Paws didn't reopen. Her husband Matthew, a trial consultant, now assists in her four businesses.

Like me, Rachel has weathered Hurricane Ian; and like me, she follows Christian values, gives back to her community and notices the collaborative spirit among business owners on Sanibel and Captiva islands.

She also came up with this interesting observation of Southwest Florida.

"I think this is a land of opportunity more than other areas," she said. "My parents moved to Southwest Florida. They have rental properties. My mom teaches art and my dad is a Florida SouthWestern State College professor. They reinvented themselves.

"If you have the work ethic, a lot can be done down here."

Entrepreneurial Mindset Q&A:

Do you feel there are a lot of opportunities for women to succeed and advance in business?

Would you rather be an entrepreneur or work for someone?

What do you do when you encounter men who are "old school."

What advice do you have in dealing with women competitors who see you as a threat?

What entrepreneurial ideas do you have?

CHAPTER 5

Marketing, Goals
And Making Money

"Today, the market rewards those that precede
their marketing efforts with the most robust
understanding of what truly matters to people."

— Earl Quenzel, marketing expert
and co-owner of Quenzel & Associates

For a decade (2011-2021), Southwest Floridians and residents from Sarasota to Tampa and upstate New York knew the name Billy Fuccillo.

And if you didn't know the name of the KIA car dealer, you knew his slogan: "It's gonna be huuuuuu-ja!"

Everything about Billy Fuccillo was huge. A former football player at the University of Syracuse, he was a big man. He smoked big cigars. He liked to party hard. His promotions included TVs and cruises.

He also was incredibly generous and philanthropic to causes, organizations and individuals where he had his 25 dealerships. As a result, the Korean-owned company recognized his Kia dealership as the world's top-seller.

"He was bigger than life," Onondaga County District Attorney William Fitzpatrick told WSTM.

My personal interactions with Billy happened when I was president of the Salvation Army of Lee, Hendry, and Glades counties. Meg Geltner, our executive director at the time, reached out to Billy for our annual Kettle Drive. He said that he would do a matching program. We ended up getting approximately $250,000 from him!

You had to hand it to him. He was a great marketer, and deep down, he was a Huuuuuuu-ja supporter of the Salvation Army! Truly, he was bigger than life! He was loud, he was boisterous, but he made an impact.

Before Billy died at age 65 in 2021, from suffering a massive stroke, he advertised. A lottttt. The owner of a marketing degree at Syracuse, Billy advertised so much he was able to negotiate ad rates down on his car commercials.

"I really believe his volume of business was not from creative (ideas), but by the sheer tonnage of media," said Earl Quenzel.

Colleen and Earl Quenzel, who have had their company, Quenzel & Associates, in Southwest Florida since 2005, have their own story to tell.

The well-known companies they worked for operated not just in millions, but in billions.

From those experiences, their marketing is based more on disseminating data and voice-of-customer research than a clever slogan, larger-than-life personality or shock value.

"There's two basic ways to double business," Earl said. "Either double your spending where everything flows into a funnel. The other way is to double the effectiveness of messaging."

The littlest details, the smallest change, can make a multi-million-dollar difference. Earl witnessed this firsthand when he worked with Priceline Europe. Its campaign was built on the slogan: Name your own price.

"We received an initial round of funding for $50 million," he said. "We launched the site. Our marketing was getting people to the website. People would put in where they wanted to go and the dates.

"We needed to get to 80 percent of people giving their credit card information to get our second round of funding. However, when we asked people to give their credit card details, we were only getting 20 percent. That is not gonna work.

"We were a month out from our second round of funding. We're struggling. The Brits are cautious. We started thinking of problems. Is the 'Name your own price' thing dodgy? We made the logo bigger. We added copy. Finally it dawned on me. Details. We changed that

Colleen and Earl Quenzel are dynamic entrepreneurs and a marketing power couple. They know how to help almost any business communicate effectively with its customers. It's a skill that all business owners must master if they want their companies to grow.

word to authorization. That empowered visitors. The next day, we came in and our metrics showed we had reached 80 percent. All that from a one-word change. From that, I became a super freak on the power of words."

In Southwest Florida, Dr. Ralph Garramone's work as a plastic surgeon looked too good to be true.

The Quenzels turned the campaign phrasing into 'A naturally youthful you,' which led Ralph Garramone to having a 49 percent annual increase in appointments.

Collen started a business in oil and gas research in Austin, Texas before moving to Houston where she worked as a stockbroker for the Paine-Webber affiliate, Rotan-Mosle. Yearning a collaborative partnership, she worked for Quality Beverage, the biggest wine & spirit distributor in the state of Texas, at that time. At Quality Beverage, she launched several new beverage brands into the marketplace, including Kendall-Jackson, Gallo Varietals, and Bacardi Breezers.

Earl worked for TWA (1984-87), Travel Channel (1987-88), Continental Airlines One Pass (1994-98) and AT&T (1994-2000), Priceline Europe (2000-2004) and South Seas Island Resort (2004-05) in a variety of marketing capacities before joining Colleen at Quenzel & Associates.

Colleen worked with airlines to come up with the concept of customers taking unused air miles and applying them toward free magazine subscriptions. Magazine publishers benefited from increased subscription numbers, which helped them charge more for advertising.

Earl and Colleen remember the days of Yellow Pages and direct mail.

They also know how social media and geo-targeting, which is location-based marketing, can help a business as well as a company website.

So detailed are Colleen and Earl's analysis and metrics that they have calculated the value of a lifetime customer.

"We look at the recency and frequency of purchases, the total monetary value and on average look at 18 months,"

Earl said. "To get the lifetime value of a customer, business owners are willing to spend one-third to acquire that customer. While some spend more, many spend less.

Colleen said watching what media perspective customers follow can lead to unpredictable outcomes.

"We worked with a men's clothing store in Naples, Florida, which catered to an upper-tier demographic," she said. "Never in our history did we see Twitter rank No. 1 in that area in social media. Every day. The ah-ha moment was that all the older Republicans were on that platform with (President Donald) Trump and all were checking out what he had to say."

That's why the numbers and data are so important. They tell a story if you're listening. Earl feels consumers buying and business people selling is an emotional transaction.

"The more someone feels a particular need or desire and the more they perceive your brand as the best possible solution to that need or desire, the bigger your brand becomes," he said. "That's what we call brand building.

"Seldom is a sale based on price, a product feature or a service benefit alone. Instead, a sale results when the totality of many factors in the buyer's mind – needs, wants, features, benefits, price, reputation – results in a favorable emotional attitude, not just toward the product or service you're marketing, but towards you ... the seller."

Advertising vs. Marketing

Earl said while advertising is more about crafting a creative message and image, marketing goes more into analytics.

One of his mentors was David Ogilvy, known as the 'Father of Advertising.' Trained at Gallup research, he was the founder of Ogilvy & Mather and led famous campaigns that included Rolls-Royce, Dove soap and Hathaway shirts.

"David used to say direct marketers made the best brand marketers because they hold themselves accountable for results," Earl said.

He also learned the value of collaboration and checking one's ego at the copy desk from Ogilvy.

"David said there's no such thing as good writers but good editors," Earl recalled. "If he was writing something important, he'd share it. When some people write something, it's your creation, you sweated over it, it's yours. He got rid of that. When he looked to have changes made on his copy, he'd hand write, 'Please improve.' That creates a space to share."

Earl often will read his ad copy out loud to hear how it sounds.

"If there's a piece of content and if Colleen doesn't understand it, very likely I'll say, 'Let's clean it up.' "

Colleen and Earl noted how we're bombarded with advertising – subtly or not – on our TVs, personal websites, social media accounts and other websites we search on.

"I'm sorting through 400 pieces of junk mail a day," Colleen said while Earl believes we're hit with 2,000 to 3,000 messages a day on various media.

He gets it.

"We're in the persuasion business," he said. "This isn't rocket science but it is hard. You're dealing with humans and human behavior. You need to be a student of human behavior."

The Power Behind Setting Goals
Recently, a young woman walked into the room and I told her, "Wow, you're beautiful. You've lost a lot of weight."

She said, "You're the first person that said that to me. I've lost 38 pounds."

My husband Tim then challenged her and said if she lost

a certain amount of weight, he'd give her $5,000.

"You're on," she said.

Now, she's thinking of setting a new goal.

My own experiences have drawn me to these girls and young ladies.

Goals have been set for everything from losing weight to making friends to making sales to buying a business. Small goals, medium goals, big goals and gigantic goals.

There has been so much research put into goal setting that corporate training materials can be bought for $600 and up.

Why? Because there has been relevant research that underlines its importance:

- Harvard study, 1979: Only 3 percent of the students of the Harvard MBA Program declared that they wrote down their goals clearly and wrote about their plans for reaching them. A total of 13 percent had goals but didn't commit them to paper. The rest of the group – 84 percent – had no definite goals at all.

  Ten years later, that 13 percent earned twice as much as the 84 percent and the 3 percent earned 10 times as much.

- In The Dream Book by Billy Cox, in its sixth printing, Gulf Coast Business Bank creator Bill Blevins read a story Zig Ziglar shared of a UCLA study that focused on people who attended the Peter Lowe Success Seminars. Those individuals who had a written goals program earned more than double those who didn't plus they were happier, healthier and got along better with family members.

"One of the things I do is sit down and dream and process those goals and then share them with our employees," Blevins said. "As we grow, I want to help our colleagues and shareholders with a profit-sharing and incentive plan where we can share the wealth and success."

- Jack Canfield made $8,000 as a Chicago teacher when he had a chat with mentor W. Clement Stone. Worth $600 million, Stone told Canfield, "I want you to set a goal that's so big that if you achieve it, you'll know it's because of the secret I am teaching you."

Canfield decided he wanted to make $100,000 that year. "I created an image of a $100,000 dollar bill and hung it on the ceiling above my bed. Every morning I'd see the image. I'd visualize what it would be like to have $100,000. Everything I did was to achieve that goal. At the end of the year, I had made $97,000."

Canfield then put a check on the ceiling worth $1 million. He came up with a book idea – Chicken Soup for the Soul. When his publisher gave him a royalty check, it was for $1 million, the highest amount any author of his had earned.

Goals Are Measurement For Success

In education from K-12, there are literally SMART Goals which can be applied to everyday life – Specific, Measureable, Achievable, Relevant and Time-Bound.

These goals break down as follows:

Specific: A narrow, focused goal that can't be confused with what the objective is.

Measurable: A specific, numerical goal.

Achievable: A goal that is realistic for the individual.

Relevant: A goal that aligns with what the individual's needs are.

Time-bound: A goal that has a deadline.

Edward Locke and Gary Latham (1990) are leaders in goal-setting theory. According to their research, goals not only affect behavior as well as job performance, but they also help mobilize energy which leads to a higher effort overall. Higher effort leads to an increase in persistent effort.

Locke and Latham also stated that there are five goal-setting principles that can help improve your chances of success. They are:

1. Clarity: This is important when it comes to goals. Setting goals that are clear and specific eliminate the confusion that occurs when a goal is set in a more generic manner.

2. Challenge: These goals help you stretch your mind and cause you to think bigger. Think of Canfield's story. This helps you accomplish more. Each success you achieve helps you build a winning mindset.

3. Commitment: This is critically important. If you don't commit to your goal with everything you have, it is less likely you will achieve it.

4. Feedback: Being open to accepting feedback keeps you on track so you know what you are doing right and and what you are doing wrong. This allows you to adjust your expectations and your plan of action going forward.

5. Task Complexity: This is the final factor. It's important to set goals that are aligned with the goal's complexity.

Let goals be your road map.

But be prepared for traffic jams, unexpected detours and forks in the road.

In other words, learn to be adaptable.

Entrepreneurial Mindset Q&A:

Do you set goals?

Do you think they're worth setting?

If you've set goals, have you set ones that you know you can make or do you shoot for the stars?

CHAPTER 6

Borrowing Money

"Once we developed a relationship and
Tom (Robinson) got comfortable with what we
are and what we're doing, he and Bill (Blevins)
took a shot on us."

– Keith Hopkins, managing partner
at Bravo Site Works

In June of 2023, Keith Hopkins found himself in a bind.

The managing partner of a burgeoning company that specializes in underground utility work for new construction projects, Hopkins flew to Pittsburgh to take part in an auction to buy needed equipment.

Then he received an email from the auction company.

"I needed to bring a letter with proof of funds or a line of credit to participate," Hopkins said. "I couldn't wait until 10 or 11 a.m. the next day or we would've missed out on lots of items to bid on."

Hopkins received the email late on a Wednesday afternoon just before closing time. While walking out of the

Pittsburgh airport gate, Hopkins spoke with Gulf Coast Business Bank employees Kelly Hart, Rosie Ruano and Thomas Robinson.

"I'm in a jam and I need help," Hopkins recalled saying.

In 19 minutes, he received a letter from Ruano, which included everything he needed.

"That wasn't great service," Hopkins said. "That was exceptional service."

That's what Robinson, senior vice president and commercial lender, and president & CEO Bill Blevins envisioned Gulf Coast Business Bank would be.

When GCBB opened in June of 2022, they became the first Southwest Florida community bank in 12 years. From 2008-2016, the FDIC had placed a virtual moratorium on de novo banks, but the reins have loosened the last few years. A de novo bank is a new bank that builds its deposit and loan customers from scratch.

Whether it's a new, upstart bank or one that has been established for decades, it's vitally important that young businesspeople and entrepreneurs establish working relationships with bankers, specifically those who borrow money.

My Banking Experiences

Early in my entrepreneurial journey, a loan officer loaned my company money for refinancing a hotel. He believed in me, and he set up some criteria in the loan that kept me on a rather short leash, but it was for my own good.

That man was Charles Idelson, who was the CEO for SunTrust. He is still my friend and we both sit on The Chapters Healthcare National Board and the Lee and Hendry County Hope Hospice Board together.

Because I developed a working relationship with Mr. Idelson

and with that bank, when I asked if I'd be able to borrow money, he replied, "For you, we can."

Being saddled with debt is difficult and stressful and can rob you of your creativity and general joy in life. So approach it carefully, and don't base your request on only the good years of income. Remember that there will be tough times, too.

Have a good backup plan. Your credit will follow you for life. Especially with young people who haven't been advised how important it is to pay your bills. Don't join a health

In building a new bank, Gulf Coast Business Bank, from the ground up, Bill Blevins, pictured left, and Thomas Robinson focused on each new customer's personal needs. And that customized approach is something all entrepreneurs should embrace in growing their brands.

club and sign a contract without looking at the fine print regarding exiting. Even if the salesperson tells you that you can get out at any time, if you sign it, it will follow you. Look over any contract very carefully. You don't want your credit to be ruined.

Purchase a car very cautiously and be sure that you can really afford it. There is insurance and maintenance, too. So, having a good backup plan is essential for everybody, whether you are an entrepreneur or not. This might sound a bit elementary for some, but I wanted to stress this just in case a student wasn't aware of the importance of good credit.

After Hurricane Charley, I had a wonderful community bank that I had been working with for five years. The eye of the hurricane came right through Captiva Island. I didn't evacuate and I stayed in my home. Several staff stayed with me and my youngest son, Erik. Everything that I owned was broken and damaged. A tornado took out my office. The National Guard patrolled the streets and helicopters flew overhead, but one guy showed up driving a jeep on the sand of the beach because of blocked roads. He came to check on his island customers, including me. It was Craig Albert, the president of the bank! The roads were blocked, but he found a way!

I actually had been hauling brush and chain-sawing. We took a water break and Craig said, "Don't worry about a thing, we have your back."

I can't tell you how much that meant to me. He worked with me and set a perfect example of a relationship banker.

At the same time, a bigger bank, which will remain unnamed, was hounding me. I didn't know what they wanted, but I gave Craig his name to call him for me and to let them know that I wasn't ignoring them. That was back in the days of pagers. That pager was going off about twice a day from my big banker. My cell phone was dead. Heck, I didn't even have an office. It was about four days after the hurricane hit. As it turned out, I had no electricity for two months and no water for one month, and they wanted me to fax them my latest financial reports. The big bank wanted an assessment of their portfolio.

They were out of touch! I asked Craig to make sure my mortgage payments were on time to that big bank. I promised myself I would refinance as soon as I could. Craig's bank took care of my home mortgage and line of credit, but the community bank's lending capabilities at that time were not big enough.

That's when I got to know Bill Blevins. He was friendly and unassuming, and we met through the Chamber of Commerce. I told him that my needs were greater than the community bank could handle. I wanted to refinance my Inn, two shopping centers, and a commercial rental house. I went to a few banks but settled on Wachovia, where he was the market president.

Years later, I knew that I would feel comfortable investing with Bill in the bank because he was meticulous and held himself up to a high standard.

We've had a working relationship for 20 years.

Importance Of Empathy

I've grown to have tremendous respect for banks, so much so that I've invested in several of them and served on the boards of directors for two of them.

My first venture was with Florida Shores Bank. We ended up merging with Stonegate Bank, which was then bought out by Centennial Bank.

The second one was Gulf Coast Business Bank, where I'm currently on the Board of Directors and on the Executive Board.

I understand that I'm not able to get a loan all the time. It's because I have sat on both sides of the table.

When loan department members show caution in loaning you money, pay attention. They may be trying to tell you it's a shaky investment. Not just from their aspect, but yours.

I never got upset and I never tried to manipulate a situation.

A bank also needs a well-rounded portfolio. This comes from the FDIC, the Federal Department of Insurance Corporation, and the bank itself.

Imagine a pie chart where a certain percentage goes to commercial loans, a certain percentage to small business owners, a certain percentage to residential loans, a certain percentage to personal lines of credit and a certain percentage to home equity lines of credit.

Sometimes the approval is based on what's available in that pie chart.

If the bank has a shortage of commercial loans but an abundance of personal lines of credit in its portfolio, it may be easier to get a commercial loan but harder to get a business loan. Or vice versa.

And when I borrow money from a bank, I don't pay off my debt a month or two after I receive it. Banks are in the business of making money, too. I don't think it's right to tie up their money and have them go through all of the work necessary for financing.

A line of credit is just that. It's meant to help a business manage cash flow and borrow from it when needed. When you're compensated for the need, you in return pay off the line of credit.

If it stays a solid loan and it doesn't fluctuate, then it's not a line of credit.

Most banks want to see it cleaned up to zero for at least one month a year, but look at the fine print and see what your bank requires. There's a lot of effort to make that loan possible.

The Business Of Banking

A bank's ability to lend is often contingent on how much money it has in deposits. The more money a bank has in deposits, the higher the ability there is to loan. That's why it's important that your business has relationships with at least two banks. The bank's lending power might have nothing to do with you, but more to do with its pie chart and how many loans to deposits that it has out there. They are in business, too.

It's like the character George Bailey in the movie It's a Wonderful Life explained how the Building & Loan department operated when people wanted to take out their life savings during a run on the bank: "You're thinking of this place all wrong as if I had the money back in a safe. The money's not here, well, it's in Joe's house, that's right next to yours and Mrs. Kennedy's house and Mrs. Makelin's house and a hundred others. You're lending them the money to build and they're going to pay it back to you as best they can. What are you going to do, foreclose on them?"

This is wise advice.

The banking crisis of 2008 and 2009 was led by a lack of investor confidence in bank solvency and declines in credit availability, which led to plummeting stock and commodity prices.

The crisis rapidly spread into a global economic shock, resulting in several bank failures. Lehman Brothers, Bear Stearns and many others closed their doors or were helped to merge with the help of regulators.

Bank of America received billions in guarantees from the government.

There were many locally. Wachovia, one of my banks, was taken over by Wells Fargo. Some banks were closing and being taken over by other banks.

As people withdrew their money, the bank's lending ability shrunk. As renewals came up, they couldn't lend.

I remember those times well. If you have a good relationship with your bankers, they will have your back to the extent the law allows them to. All files must be backed up with the most up-to-date information.

So, when your bank asks for updated records, they must comply with the regulations.

They are not picking on you, but merely following the rules. The regulators come in and stay for several weeks, going over every file.

I hope this helps you understand that banking is a two-way relationship.

Once you get the loan, it doesn't stop there. Bill Blevins, president of Gulf Coast Business Bank, previously was the market president for Wachovia. It went from a large bank to a huge bank.

The lending practices have changed a lot. The hometown relationship banking was put to the test. Bill moved on to another bank.

I believe the temporary setback was the best thing to happen to him. It led Bill to where he is today.

While this was happening, I was on the Board of Florida Shores Bank. I encouraged him, saying one day, he might consider starting a bank of his own.

Little did I know, but others were whispering to him as well. Bill Valenti, a mutual friend, not only offered suggestions but also mentored Bill through the process.

Timing is everything, and Bill waited until the timing was right.

Building Relationships

When Keith Hopkins confided in his mentors for the better part of two decades, they told him one of the keys to success was having a relationship with a local banker who "knows who you are and takes you seriously."

Hopkins found that out the hard way when he lost out on a life-changing deal because he couldn't get the funding.

"I was treated like a second-class citizen," he said. "It was extremely frustrating. And a lot of pain.

"I have a bachelor's in finance and an MBA in entrepreneurial studies and international business. In our two years, a lot of our profits have gone back into our business. But banks only cared for me at an earned-income level."

Hopkins met Robinson through a mutual friend. They shared a love of bourbon, which Hopkins includes in his barbecues. He then shared his frustrations.

"We couldn't grow without more capital," Hopkins said. "Once we developed a relationship and Tom got comfortable with what we are and what we're doing, he and Bill took a shot on us."

Gulf Coast Business Bank started Hopkins' company – Bravo Site Networks – with a $100,000 line of credit. Once that line was amortized out, they received another line for $250,000.

That investment is working for both sides.

Hopkins said his young business made $1.5 million after Year 1 and continues to grow.

He has seven crews working job sites across Florida from Naples to Palmetto, 130 miles away.

"I'm crushing it," Hopkins said. "I have these contracts and they're seeing the $100,000 wires and checks coming in. We once again turned back to Tom and Bill at Gulf Coast Business Bank to provide the capital to expand into our third line of business - wet utilities, sewer, water and storm drainage.

"As we enter this arena, the stakes become significantly higher as the average contract value we are pursuing is between $1 million and $4 million, which will require additional working capital to properly execute. At this level, both our bonding company and the general contractors we are bidding for are closely scrutinizing our balance sheet as they evaluate our access to working capital."

Because of the challenges with bigger or more established banks as well as credit unions, Blevins and Robinson want – and need – to know their customers' dreams and goals to build stronger relationships.

Robinson said knowing the customers' backgrounds and what they aspire to achieve helps them determine who to invest in.

"We're a small community bank that lends to small businesses and startups," Robinson said. "We can't afford to make mistakes for our customers and shareholders."

Because of that, Robinson said he looks at the three Cs – character, collateral and cash flow.

He also needs to look a borrower in the eyes.

"When I get a call from Chicago or Wisconsin and it sounds great, I say, 'When are you going to come to town?' Until I see the whites of their eyes, I'm not lending."

The Art Of Borrowing

Mike Martin, former president of FGCU, once told the story of a successful farmer's philosophy on working with bankers. The farmer made the comment that when he borrowed a couple of hundred thousand dollars, the bank was in control of his loan. But when the farmer borrowed a couple of million dollars, he was in control. The bankers literally couldn't afford for the farmer to fail. So they worked closely together. Something to keep in mind.

Also, remember if you become a highly successful businessman – again, we're talking millions here – you can borrow from yourself.

My husband Tim Younquist is a master at it.

"I'll never cash the stock, I'll borrow from it," he said. "Most places allow you to borrow up to 85 percent of your equity. We never borrow more than 50 percent."

Tim understands compound interest. He also understands that if the money borrowed pays for itself and then some, it can essentially bring a higher yield than what his stock was making.

"When you can borrow for less than half of what you can get from a bank, then life gets easier," he said. "I don't need the financial help from a bank and that lets you think of different ways to run your business."

So whether a person is a millionaire, multi-millionaire, decamillionaire, centimillionaire or billionaire, their mindset is different. Those are a lot of names to describe various levels of money, right?

The one common thing is to keep a good relationship with your banker. You never know when you might need them.

According to Business Insider, one of the key strategies employed by the ultrawealthy to keep their tax bills low is to borrow money. They finance their lavish lifestyles by using their fortunes as collateral for loans, which can come with single-digit interest rates, according to ProPublica and independent experts.

Building A Team

Bill Blevins, who has 30-plus years of experience working at community, regional and national banks, said most people need to work with two banks – one community and one regional. The recession of 2007 to 2009 taught him this lesson to pass along to clients.

He felt the timing was right for a de novo and that community banks fill a need.

"We've put together a good team," Blevins said. "We have a good board of directors. One-third are from Collier County, Florida, and two-thirds are from adjacent Lee County. I'll never be the smartest guy in the room, but if you've got good people around you, it's easy to be successful."

It wasn't a cakewalk to raise the money. Many people still hold onto the memories of the bank failures of 2008 and 2009. Others realized the change, with the low interest rates, was an excellent time to start raising capital.

When Gulf Coast Business Bank formed and a board was created, there was a lot of strategy – and intentionality – involved.

There's a reason why the words Business Bank are right in the name of GCBB.

Entrepreneurs and small businesses are the backbone of our whole country and bankers need to have relationships with those people.

When the GCBB board was formed, key players in the community were sought out who worked closely with entrepreneurs and small businesses.

By bringing together like-minded people who fit in and complement each other, the bank built a strong leadership team that was fine-tuned along the way.

Part of Gulf Coast Business Bank's mission statement is that it's "made up of a group of motivated community leaders whose purpose and commitment is to help clients focus and achieve their dreams and goals."

Bill has led the way and with a great staff in place, he set up some key fundamentals of the organization. You need to have a vision and a mission.

Banking is about establishing relationships, building relationships and growing relationships.

Investors backed Bill and the original board members. There were 284 investors in Collier and Lee counties who helped raise $23.6 million. We have investor gatherings all over the two-county region, and we surpassed our goal, but we had to turn down some investors.

The state regulators did not allow us to do more than our approved plan. We were now in business. The bank has now grown to $100 million in deposits in two years. We are on track with our success plan.

"Our position is to be a vital lifeline in the community, offer personal service to local businesses that they cannot and will not get from national banks where they are but a number," Bill said.

Entrepreneurial Mindset Q&A:

Do you have a go-to place to borrow money? How were you able to do that?

Did you take out a loan to pay for college? How did you accomplish that?

If you had a great business idea, who would you pitch it to?

How confident are you that you could get an investor to buy in?

How confident are you that a bank would give you a loan?

CHAPTER 7

Balancing Faith, Family And Business

"For the love of money is the root of all kinds
of evils. It is through this craving that some
have wandered away from the faith and
pierced themselves with many pangs."

— 1 Timothy 6:10

Can God, business, family and making money co-exist?

Some of you may say yes, others no and others may say you don't care.

I think you should care.

Can you serve two masters – God and money?

I believe that God and money can co-exist. I believe that family and business can co-exist, especially when loved ones are part of your business.

Dr. Aysegul Timur, the president at Florida Gulf Coast University, and my fellow entrepreneurs also will share their views.

Money And Family

You can find many verses in the Bible related to family:

> **1 Timothy 5:8:** But if anyone does not provide for his relatives, and especially for members of his household, he has denied the faith and is worse than an unbeliever.

> **Luke 12:48:** To whom much is given, much will be required.

To me, this verse means that we are responsible for what we have and should use our talents of knowledge, time, money and leadership to help benefit others, including family members.

After my nephew Corban worked for me as manager of my Inn, I saw his entrepreneurial spirit. He was working for me, but he also wanted to make items to sell and was researching different ways to make money other than being an hourly employee. I knew that he wanted to grow.

At the same time, I had a pizza restaurant that was breaking even. It was a small business and I had to hire people to do everything. The only way that business was going to thrive was to have an owner/manager, so I gave him my pizza restaurant and he now is one of my tenants where he owns Captiva Island Pizza. I gave him the equipment, but when it broke, he needed to fix it or replace it. He pays rent to me for the location and it's a win-win.

I taught him basics like counting his pizza boxes. Corban went through some challenges but he persevered like I hoped he would. He rolled up his sleeves and is doing well enough that he could buy the car he wanted. Keep counting the pizza boxes, Corban!

My grandson Tristen Brown and his girlfriend, Cora, also helped me get two of my businesses back open as we did hurricane restoration after Hurricane Ian devastated the region in September 2022.

Two years after the storm, I still had Keylime Bistro on Captiva Island to open and Latte Da Coffee & Ice Cream to open.

In late September 2024, Hurricane Helene hit us with a powerful storm surge that flooded all of my properties with the exception of the Keylime Bistro on Boca Grande. Located in the Historic Train Station, it fared well because of its Concrete Block Stucco exterior and higher elevations. We had just reopened all of our

My grandson, Tristen Brown, and his girlfriend, Cora Rafferty, have become part of the management team at Stilwell Enterprises.

properties on Captiva Island when Hurricane Milton came two weeks later in early October 2024. Again, all of our businesses were flooded, but this time the Boca Grande location also flooded! Talk about a setback!

When you experience a storm surge, it brings a thick muddy muck that is very thick, slippery and stinky. So we were back to hurricane clean up and recovery once again. I was quoted by The News-Press as saying, "There is a light at the end of the tunnel, but right now I'm in the tunnel." Again, my management team and I worked together to get things back open as soon as we could.

Ten of my units in The Captiva Island Inn needed to be rebuilt due to storm damage.

I look forward to working with Tristen and seeing what path he takes. This will be a good way to see if he enjoys management or not.

It'll be good for Tristen to be on his own. I think the key will be for me to listen and allow him to go on his own path, whatever that may be.

I don't want him to feel boxed in. I want this to be their decision, and I want to let them find their own way as everyone must find the path that's right for them.

These similar Bible verses are related to abundance, prosperity and financial success:

2 Corinthians 9:8: And God is able to bless you abundantly, so that in all things at all times, having all that you need, you will abound in every good work.

Deuteronomy 28:12: The LORD will open the heavens, the storehouse of his bounty, to send rain on your land in season and to bless all the work of your hands. You will lend to many nations but will borrow from none.

Proverbs 28:25: A greedy man stirs up strife, but the one who trusts in the Lord will be enriched.

Psalm 128:2: You shall eat the fruit of the labor of your hands; you shall be blessed, and it shall be well with you.

There also are a lot of Bible verses related to money:

Hebrews 13:5: Keep your life free from the love of money, and be content with what you have, for he has said, "I will never leave you nor forsake you."

Matthew 6:24: No one can serve two masters, for either he will hate the one and love the other, or he will be devoted to the one and despise the other. You cannot serve God and money.

Proverbs 22:7: The rich rules over the poor, and the borrower is the slave of the lender.

Ecclesiastes 5:10: He who loves money will not be satisfied with money, nor he who loves wealth with his income; this also is vanity.

Please note from the above Bible verses that money wasn't the root of all evil; it was love of it.

As long as your daily motivator when you wake up isn't, "Today I'm going to make a lot of money," but rather living your life with God in control, you can make all kinds of money. "Use me today, God."

When we go to work with a servant's attitude of providing goods or services that will help others accomplish their goals, that's a good start.

In my case, providing a place to vacation or to dine so others can unwind from their hectic lives while on vacation is my noble goal in giving back to society. We provide a service even if it's just a day trip to the island.

If we are good managers when providing that service, we will usually make money.

Of course, there are things that can happen, but I'm talking about a mindset.

With the motivation of only making money, you'll never be satisfied. Why, you might ask? Because no matter how much you have, somebody will always have more. You'll spend your life on an exhausting treadmill, leaving you exhausted and empty inside.

My mom and dad, Ellie and Tom Kolar, seated, at my mother's 90th birthday party celebration with their three children, standing from left to right, Beverly, Tom and me.

And if the focus is only to make money, you won't have time to spend it on yourself, your friends, your family or a cause that could help your community.

Instead, I have focused on trying to make a difference. I want to leave this life with the knowledge that I didn't waste my life on frivolous pursuits but in attempting to help others.

Other Views

It has been a whirlwind for Aysegul Timur, who became FGCU president on May 4, 2023.

When she was asked about balance, she said, "Ahhhh... It is a hard question.

"I have my FGCU family and I have my core family. Sometimes, it's so difficult. I'm so passionate about my job I can spend hours at it.

"However, I'm also very self-aware when I realize, 'OK, I'm going too much in one direction.' When these things happen, I know how to back off.

"I have a 16-year-old girl. One Saturday, I'm home and I planned to spend all day at work. But it was a beautiful day and I realized time won't come back. I'm going to spend the day with my daughter and I can get things done the next day."

President Timur said mentors have told her the importance of having three-day weekends for balance as well as mental health. So does her husband Mete.

"My husband says, 'Ok, it's time. I'm booking a weekend.' That family time is important. It's important to create self-awareness or you can burn yourself out. And I love those three days. It's so refreshing. I also can see things from a 30,000-foot view."

Brian Rist, former Storm Smart owners and FGCU professor, said he tells students that if their goals in starting businesses are focused too much on making money, they likely won't be sustainable.

"It should be to make the world a better place, solve problems and help people," he said.

Because he can do Zoom calls and conference calls, Brian avoids having to travel, which would take him from family for days at a time. He also added that the reason he became an entrepreneur was that he could make more time for his family once he sold Storm Smart.

"There were times I'd be gone four or five nights out of the week and my wife would take care of the home," he said. "I really appreciated that. Now, we have the rewards of selling our business, traveling and doing what we want."

My husband Tim, who has worked with brother Harvey for decades, simply said, "If we don't both agree on a project, we don't do it."

Rachel Pierce went so far as to say she'd sell her four businesses in a heartbeat if it meant choosing between her work and her children. She did add that husband Matthew having a successful job makes that choice easy.

"Balance, I get asked that question every single day," Rachel said. "I don't work in all the stores much. In a pinch, I will be the backup for the backup.

"What I do is hire the right people, pay them well and trust them to do their jobs. All those who work for me are very loyal."

By working hard, leading by example and listening to her employees, Rachel said she doesn't micromanage while learning about their strengths and goals.

"We have a woman who worked for Ann Taylor so she does all the displays and it's been fun to see what she does," Rachel said. "It's cool to see what people's skill sets are and whether they could thrive when put in that position. I do like to know what their passions are."

Maybe young people have it figured out.

Dr. Alise Bartley, who has studied mental health for 30 years, said many young people have placed less importance on their careers and more on a work-life balance, which has forced employers to adjust.

"We were part of the parents of the Greatest Generation, right?," Dr. Bartley said. "The real focus was on success and worth and who you are professionally.

"Today's generation is 'No, no, no, I work so I can have a roof over my head; and as long as I get most of my needs met, I'm fine. It's a shift."

But for those young people who are laser focused on goals of success and worth and drive, the passion that can push them through hard times can also cause issues.

"Passion has a consequence if you push too hard," Bartley said. "Your spouse may say, 'I can't do this anymore' if you're missing dinners, not being there with the kids, not being there for him or her.

"In the world of work, people can control their environment so they choose to stay at work."

Final Thoughts

Are you living your life to please others or to please God?

My walk is to live my life, seeking His guidance and direction. It takes off all of the pressure of doing it on my own. It's all in His hands and frees me to work hard and not fret.

I just put one foot in front of the other and keep going. I ask for Him to block my way if I'm headed in the wrong direction. Sometimes He has done just that.

I encourage you to find balance in your life. It can't be all work or all play; it can't be all about the children and leave your other relationships lacking. It can't be all about your friends and leave other things lacking.

If you are into exercise, it can't be all working out, or you'll burn yourself out. It's really just finding your personal balance.

What works for one person, might not work as well for another. Take the time to sit back and listen in the

My two sons, Erik Brown, pictured to my left, with Chauncey Brown. Grandsons Tristen, front left, and Ethan Brown in June 2012.

quietness of the day or night. When faced with a decision, listen to your heart. Meditate, and in that quietness, often things are revealed. My driving time is precious because I'm in a world of thoughts and prayers.

Find a good mentor or friend. This can help you in many ways. It might be as simple as bouncing an idea off them. They might see things from a different perspective.

However, select your friends carefully and wisely. Don't take your relationships for granted, whether it's your spouse, partner or friend. Relationships are very pliable, much like a rubber band. They will snap back when stretched, but eventually, they will snap or break if taken advantage of and pushed and pulled too much.

Be quick to thank people. Having an attitude of gratitude is so much more appealing than one who keeps wanting and asking for more.

And for goodness sake, let us all forget the word entitled. We are not entitled to anything.

Entrepreneurial Mindset Q&A:

Do you think you have the proper balance in your life?

If you don't have the balance you're seeking, what changes do you need to make?

Do you have a favorite Bible phrase when it comes to family?

Do you have a favorite Bible phrase when it comes to money?

If you have started or want to start a new business, what would your mission statement be?

PART 1: Notes

PART 2:
The Sandy Side Of Business

CHAPTER 8

From Windy City To Breezy Beaches

"I got up first thing in the morning. Kenny
Schwartz came in with coffee and donuts.
We started talking about jobs and stuff and
I asked, 'Is there somewhere to build
cabinets?' Kenny said, 'I don't know about
that but we could use somebody for public
relations. We could use you.
We pay $1.30 to $1.40 an hour.' "

- Tom Kolar on his first day after
moving to Cape Coral in 1960

Do you come from a family of adventurers?

Were your parents willing to move from one part of the
country to another so they and their children could have a
better life?

Mine did. My parents, Ellie and Tom Kolar, have been
entrepreneurs almost their entire adult lives.

They married in 1951.

When my dad went into the Army, he bought this beautiful 1950 white Cadillac convertible. My parents made a bold step but knew that they could rent the car out once in a while. They were based in sunny Santa Maria, California and he became friendly with his Army cohorts.

While my dad took the bus, he rented the car out to the young men who wanted to go on dates. This helped pay for gas and car payments. He knew credit was important so he didn't miss payments.

One time, my dad and his fellow Army buddies found out they were moving to Camp Carson in Colorado Springs, Colorado. They needed to get their trunks to Colorado and my father realized this was a perfect opportunity to make some money, so he and my mom loaded up six of their foot lockers into this Cadillac convertible. With all sorts of items sticking out of the convertible, it looked like the opening for the hilarious 1960s comedy show Beverly Hillbillies. Dad just hoped it didn't rain.

The hot trip exhausted them so they splurged and stayed in a hotel. They loaded all of the lockers into their room for safety. The pool provided recreation.

I always think about how much they pushed and stretched themselves but they knew they could do it. I think that's the confidence that they instilled in me so I could stretch myself and think of clever ways to bring in added revenue.

Once my dad left the Army, they started a custom cabinet business and built our first home.

When my parents attended a Chicago boat show at the old Union Stockyards in 1958, this started a new adventure. They moved from the Midwest to Florida's Gulf Coast. Their excursion would be filled with new opportunities, varied challenges and lasting legacies.

Even at age 2, I have memories of my parents. The experiences and stories have stayed with me and are a guiding light as I travel on my own entrepreneurial journey.

Go South Young Couple

Whether it was a way to get out of the cold or enjoy one of their passions – boating – my parents attended the boat show with an open mind. They may have joked they attended like two dummies but I think they sought a different life.

The cabinetry business they built ground to a halt during Chicago's winter months when construction slowed. Their only connections were with contractors.

At the Stockyards, Gulf American Land Corporation owners Leonard and Jack Rosen set up a booth featuring Cape Coral, Florida. They called it the water wonderland of the world. Naturally, the literature said that Cape Coral had more canals and waterways than Venice, Italy.

With 103 square miles of Cape Coral land bought, the Rosens made a huge investment.

The early days of Cape Coral, Florida, where the sign read: Cape Coral – A Waterfront Wonderland.

Hall of Fame broadcaster Bill Stern, who announced the nation's first remote sports broadcast and the first telecast of a baseball game, was Gulf American's spokesman.

Now my dad is the outgoing one. He's a very hard worker who finds humor in everything. He's quick to admit when he makes mistakes. He's approachable and authentic and doesn't take life too seriously, yet he still could be focused and driven.

My mom, she's the quiet one. She's also graceful, kind, guarded in her words and thoughtful. Numbers-driven, she's the substance and conscience behind my dad's ideas, the accountant who watches the incoming and outgoing. She'd work until the middle of the night.

In the summer of 1959, they initially traveled to Florida by boat. My sister Beverly and I joined them for part of the journey, but our grandparents picked us up within the first day because they feared for our safety when they saw the extreme water traffic on the Mississippi River. After that, our parents resumed their trip.

Too Good To Pass Up

After selling their home business in Chicago, my parents moved to Cape Coral around Easter, 1960.

When Kenny Schwartz, the Rosens' vice president and general manager, offered my dad a job upon arriving in town, he took it.

He had various tasks, one of which included waving down passing motorists and calling them VITs – Very Important Travelers.

I fondly remember him sharing one of his ideas to get people to stop. He decided to paint yellow lines on the road, which led cars into the Gulf American parking lot.

How funny!

Of course, city officials made him paint them black again, but it was clever and showed his bosses how innovative he could be.

Once they pulled over, the VITs received Florida-squeezed orange juice, a map and information about Cape Coral.

My father, Tom Kolar, in his security guard uniform when he and my mom first arrived in Cape Coral. I believe he was Gulf American's first security officer in Cape Coral and deputized, before his hard work made him a vice president.

Meanwhile, the Rosens flew prospective customers into Page Field where they had a fleet of 23 buses to transport buyers to their vast holdings, according to The News-Press. They also gave prospects vouchers for hotel stays, which later became helpful for my parents.

Our family commitment to each other is something that makes me extremely proud.

Not long after my parents moved, my grandparents followed. They sold their restaurant and truck stop and bought the Memory Lane Cottages on Fort Myers Beach, Florida, which is the Lighthouse Resort Inn and Suites today.

Getting Involved In Cape Coral

My parents became entrenched in the community. Before my brother came along, my mom ran the bait shop at the Cape Coral Yacht Club. My dad, who had a huge respect for the military, also became a Cape Coral deputy.

Advertisements featured my parents. They were a good-looking young couple and represented the all-American family.

My dad promoted property for the Rosens, who flew in prospective customers. Local realtors provided competition and aggressively tried to sway those customers almost as soon as they departed the plane.

The realtors would shout that they could sell prospective buyers land for less. To cool off some of the aggression, Gulf American employees turned on the sprinklers by the sales center. The salesmen would open their umbrellas as they continued their relentless efforts.

Some of the newer realtors and salesmen at Gulf American could be real wheeler-dealers. To avoid buyer's remorse from any salesperson's false promises, the Rosens and my dad came up with the idea of putting up cameras and speakers in rooms to monitor the realtors' and salesmen's presentations and responses. They were being held accountable for what they said – and offered.

Pressure Builds On Everyone

My father made regular drives across Florida to Miami, Lake Wales, River Ranch and Port of The Islands, and he also took regular flights to Tombstone and Tucson, Arizona on company business for almost nine years.

Stress and pressure started to physically affect him. His neck would get tight while in a car or on a plane. It bothered him so much he used a harness or cushioned sling strapped for his neck and head. The harness was then attached to a rope and pulley system over a door. My dad didn't complain, he just did it.

As my dad worked his way up in the company to vice president, my mom got involved in bridge and golf and also was our Girl Scout leader. My brother was the first boy born in Cape Coral, arriving in 1962.

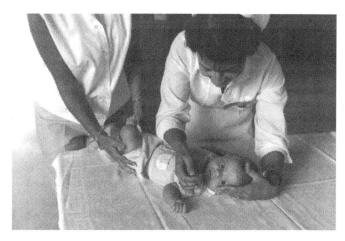

My brother, Tom Kolar Jr., was the first baby boy born in Cape Coral on July 16, 1962.

The Rosens may have hit the jackpot but they also had stress. Leonard's brother, Jack, died in 1969, the same year their $678,000 investment in Cape Coral turned into $150 million in stock.

My dad felt he needed a fresh start and a new career. He didn't want to be away from family so much. He also was about to fulfill a dream.

I always knew my mom and dad were saving for something, I just didn't know what. My mom was very frugal. Regularly, we ate tuna and hot dogs. We didn't waste anything and we rarely ate out. My mom sewed most of our clothes.

My grandparents, Clarence and Esther Roessler, are standing in front of the Memory Lane Motel, which is now called the Lighthouse Island Resort and is owned by my brother and his wife, Tom and Melinda Kolar.

When my parents bought a one-story, eight-room motel called The Eventide Motel on Fort Myers Beach with a partner, I was totally surprised. I didn't realize that they had saved so much money. It was right across the street from Uncle Kelly and Aunt Jane's diner called the Tradewinds Cafe.

My parents sold that eight-room motel to my grandparents and moved it to Memory Lanes Cottages. Literally. They had it raised on pilings, cut it in half and moved it a half mile. My grandmother built her laundry facility and a large party room underneath. This often is where we would gather with family and friends.

There was now an empty lot, which my parents used to build a 39-unit motel. They kept the Eventide Motel name. Many years later, it became a Ramada Inn. Eventually, the Ramada Inn was torn down to make room for the beachside part of the Margaritaville Hotel. The postcard had a detail description of the Eventide Motel, which read:

> Thirty-nine Motel-Apartments and Deluxe Efficiency Suites all with an unrestricted view of the Gulf of Mexico, located with more than 200 feet of white sand beach. All deluxe efficiency suites have a living room, two Bahama lounges, large fully-equipped electric kitchens, baths with showers and tubs, one bedroom (two double beds), TV, private balcony overlooking the Gulf, individually heated and air conditioned. Wall-to-wall carpeting and beautifully decorated. Can accommodate 6 persons. Heated pool.
>
> Sailing, Fishing and Swimming on our own beach. Public fishing pier and playground. Restaurants, Supermarket, Post Office, Gift Shops, Beauty &

Barber Shops, Pharmacy, Laundromat, Bicycle & Boat rentals and Cocktails all within walking distance. Nearby you may enjoy Golf, Bowling, Deep Sea Fishing, and Dog Racing. Just about everything you need for a pleasant vacation.

Your Hosts – TOM & ELLIE KOLAR

Family Comes Together

I remember helping my dad build a spiral staircase, which led to an upstairs with a kitchen. That's where we lived.

We had hoped to open the motel by November or December when winter visitors arrived; but delays pushed construction back to the end of the season.

Making ends meet was difficult that year. We rented rooms for $12 per night. Thank goodness, we received checks from Gulf American as reimbursement for vouchers they gave prospective clients.

To make ends meet, we did such things as putting bottles of Winn-Dixie Chek soda in the Pepsi machine. We could buy 10 bottles for $1 and sell each bottle for a profit. Feeling sorry for a young family, the Pepsi distributor never said a word that first year. He knew we were struggling.

To cut expenses, my parents sold our home and we moved into the motel. That helped a lot because we lived right there and we could do everything together.

I cleaned rooms, helped do repairs and worked at the front desk. As a family, we all did our part.

In 1973, I ran the hotel for a week when my parents went on vacation. Because I was 17, my sister and her husband moved in. I loved the responsibility and they loved being able to take a break from day-to-day work.

By 1974, my parents were on solid footing. They traveled

to Europe and went on vacations for a month with my grandparents.

It was great having my grandparents so close by at their Memory Lane Cottages. They received money from the state when a bridge connecting Fort Myers Beach to Fort Myers ran right through their cottage court. So the family went from struggling to doing very well.

By then I had a few years' worth of experiences, experiences that stoked my entrepreneurial fires.

Thank you, Mom, Dad, Grandma, Grandpa, Uncle Kelly and Aunt Jane.

The front of the postcard promoting the Eventide Motel.

Entrepreneurial Mindset Q&A:

Did your parents or family members ever leave their home for a potentially better opportunity?

Would you have the courage to leave your home for a better life?

When faced with adversity like Ellie and Tom did, what would you do?

If your children wanted a job, how old would they have to be before you allowed it?

CHAPTER 9

A Life Shaped By Age 10

"The kindest people are not born that way,
they are made. They are the ones that have
experienced so much at the hands of life, they
are the ones who have dug themselves out
of the dark, who have fought to turn every
loss into a lesson. The kindest people do
not just exist – they choose to soften where
circumstance has tried to harden them, they
choose to believe in goodness, because they
have seen firsthand why compassion is so
necessary. They have seen firsthand
why tenderness is so important in this world."

– Bianca Sparacino

So many good things have happened to me. When you meet
someone with a level of success, it's very easy to assume
that they've lived a privileged life and haven't had to
struggle like most people.

Perhaps they inherited it or took over the family business.

When looking at me, you might see all of the outside things, but the inside matters the most.

You would see a marriage to Tim Youngquist, a good and generous man, with a family who accepts me and appreciates me. We live in a nice house and have a great lifestyle.

I have two handsome sons, Chauncey and Erik, loving parents and siblings, who are not only my siblings but also my friends. Tim and I have five children and 12 grandchildren.

We have terrific friends with whom to work with in charities, business dealings and partnerships. We travel and go boating together; when you see us, we are usually in a large group.

The restaurants that I own are in my favorite resort destinations, and I have many devoted staff.

I've received numerous awards. Junior Achievement Business Hall of Fame. Lifetime Achievement Award from Gulf Coast Business and others.

When you read these paragraphs above and see these compliments, many may think I've had this perfect life with miles of smiles and no conflicts or challenges.

Have I had a wonderful life? Yes.

But perfect? No way.

It's through adversity that true strength is built. I've had a lot of adversity, but if I had the ability to go back and change it, I likely wouldn't change a thing.

The times when you're challenged the most are the times when you can gain clarity. Since I'm very God-driven, it is the time when I'm the very weakest that God speaks to me and gives me direction. I am hoping that by sharing a bit, it might help others.

Rather than being blindsided by adversity when it comes your way, just expect it.

Life is full of adversity. Don't let it pull you under. Instead, look for the lesson in it and figure out how to turn it into something good. Something better, stronger and more resilient.

Sometimes during the roughest challenges, I've spoken aloud and called out to God asking for a sign:

"God, please give me your wisdom and direction! I don't want anything that you don't want for me. I come to you with total trust and faith with a willingness to do one thing – to follow your direction. Just send me a clear sign. I'm so distracted right now; it must be almost written in the sky!"

Guess what has happened? He has sent a sign.

Sometimes it's not what I expected. And sometimes the sign has been so clear that I've occasionally stopped dead in my tracks.

Sometimes it has been cutting off a business transaction. It might be as simple as not allowing that toxic person to bring you down. Moving away from those situations takes strength.

There have been other times when I think I missed God's sign and made a mistake. But with faith, I must trust that going down that wrong road was all for a reason. So, I'm literally walking in faith.

And that's hard because life is hard. And cruel sometimes.

I've been betrayed.

I've had marriages end.

I've lost two babies.

I've been body shamed.

I've been accosted.

I've had my life threatened.

I've dealt with the mental illness of a loved one.

I've dealt with years of my youngest son's drug and alcohol addiction.

I've had businesses heavily damaged by hurricanes.

I've had to shut down a business that wasn't performing as planned.

And I've had people try to undermine me in various ventures.

Some of these situations happened when I was young, others when I was vulnerable, another when I thought of slowing down a bit.

Emotional Trauma

Every adversity has a start; and for me it began at age 10. I visited my cousin and there was a neighbor down the street who invited some neighborhood children to come and swim in his pool.

It was the only pool in the entire neighborhood and my aunt thought the neighbor was just wonderful. He came across as nice and never did anything out of line, but in hindsight, I should have trusted my instincts because I felt a bit of caution with him.

The next year I visited my cousin again for a week and there were even more children swimming at the neighbor's pool.

When I went inside to use the bathroom, that was when it happened. Nobody missed me because there were so many children in the pool playing.

I was sexually abused. My cousin saw that I was crying, and she asked me if I was okay.

That moment helped define who I am. I should have listened to my intuition. I learned some difficult lessons, lessons that I carry with me today.

I first went through a variety of emotions.

I had an anger toward that man, which I carried for the next seven years.

Adding to the anger was fear. Because that neighbor threatened my family's life, I told no one. I held it inside.

However, my mind was strong, and I understood I had to take things into my own hands. If my dad knew, he would go to jail for harming that man. After all, he was an Army Ranger and taught hand-to-hand combat.

So, I kept it in.

The next summer, without saying why, I told my parents I never wanted to return where I would be remotely close to my cousin and her awful neighbor.

"I don't see myself going there anymore," I said. "I'd rather work and be with you."

My closest friend saw a change but I dealt with it by keeping busy.

It was at that time that I got busy working for my aunt and uncle at their café as a dishwasher.

They would pick me up around 5 a.m. and we drove to Fort Myers Beach from Cape Coral. After work at 2 p.m. I would walk over to my grandparents' cottages, and I helped my grandmother take down the laundry from the clothesline. She did all the sheets and towels for 65 cottages and there was always something that needed attention.

My grandparents worked 12- and 14-hour days. But they also knew how to have fun. My grandmother's laugh was contagious, and friends and family always knew that they were welcome. It was the place to go and have fun with potluck barbecues, playing billiards on their pool table or taking a dip in their swimming pool.

Through all the busy work, I still had an ache in my stomach that wouldn't go away.

At first, I mistook it for hunger. Then I looked in the mirror and didn't like what I saw.

I hated conflict and to this day, I really do my best to stay away from it. I learned to mask my real feelings and I learned to fib. Fib is a nice word for a lie.

I just told people what they wanted to hear so there wouldn't be conflict.

But with each fib, the ache was worse, and I wasn't liking myself at all. I experienced an inner dread.

As I worked through my anger and dread, I put this invisible, protective bubble around myself by working, helping, pleasing and thinking.

Good Deeds

I helped my grandparents, relatives and parents with their businesses. Doing all the tasks they asked, doing them well and getting praised made me feel so good. I thrived on praise because that was the only way that I would like myself.

When taking the school bus to Cypress Lake Middle School, I saw bullies picking on a girl who didn't have shoes. I took my extra pair of shoes, put them in a backpack and gave them to the girl, who returned them to me before she departed the bus.

I didn't do that for praise, I did it because I had empathy.

Because the girl's parents didn't accept handouts, we continued this ritual for a while. It brought me joy to help her. She didn't know it, but she was helping me like myself a bit more.

To this day, I think that random act of kindness is what started me on my journey to help others and hopefully leave this world a better place. We moved to the beach, and I no longer rode the bus with her, but we would see one another passing in the hallways until we graduated from high school.

About the same time that I helped this girl, my mother complimented my looks. She often said, "Sandy always has been a good helper, Sandy always has been motivated."

But on this day, my mom looked at me and said, "You've turned into such a beautiful young lady. Your hair looks so pretty, and I didn't have to help you with anything."

I firmly believe when you do something good for somebody, we receive far more than we give. It also keeps the positive vibes going.

My mom's words lit up my life. I was almost speechless. I had to leave so my mom wouldn't see the tears. Joyful tears. Back to the bubble.

When my parents left for vacations and left me in charge of the hotel in my teens, I felt so needed. Sometimes, guests would be a bit excessive in what they asked for; but never liking conflict and wanting to please, I'd accommodate their requests.

I tended to put a Band-Aid over a splinter in business when things became uncomfortable; but over time, I worked through that, too, and became more assertive.

I also kept my mind occupied. I thought of owning my own business as a teenager. I thought of owning a hotel. I thought of helping others.

I got bored easily so I kept thinking. It also kept me from being alone with my thoughts.

Pace Center For Girls

One thing I didn't have a tolerance for was bullying. I didn't like people who put down people and criticized them. Kids can be so cruel, and it seemed like there were a lot of them in my middle and high school years. A lot of kids felt they were better, so they tried to put down other kids. It's really their inner ugliness coming out or a way of hiding their own insecurities.

Maybe that's why I felt a connection to Pace Center For Girls in my adulthood.

Since 1985, Pace Center has been on a mission to find the great in every girl. Pace Center also protects these girls from bullies.

It helps so much when young people are praised.

Motivating others brings joy. Try it. It's not about the next business deal or the next acquisition, it's that feeling when you know that you've done something right or good.

My own experiences have drawn me to these girls and young ladies.

At Pace Center, we had a heartbreaking mentoring session.

When a middle school-aged girl shared that her stepdad had assaulted her, she said that there was no point in bringing it all out. If her stepdad went to jail, who would pay the bills? Then I remembered from when she shared her story that she had a little sister. I asked, "Do you think she is safe?" It was like a lightbulb went off. She asked the staff to call the police.

The stepfather was arrested, and this brave young girl saved her sister from a lifetime of having to overcome the aftereffects of abuse.

We must protect our children and the reality is, sometimes we don't see the signs.

Sometimes things just happen. We must try our best to protect them. At Pace, it's the counseling component that helps the girls get their life back on track after something in their life got them off track. They are good girls that just need a little direction and somebody to love them and listen to them and guide them. It's so rewarding to see girls that have come with lots of anger turn into beautiful young adults.

Not all have the same story. Some have parents who have addiction problems, some have parents in jail, some might be victims of bullying and some might have gotten in trouble with the law.

Now Is What's Important!

Just remember: If you've struggled, what you were isn't what you are or what you can be. As long as you are alive, walking, talking, thinking and doing, you have the chance to make an impact.

Own your life. All of it. The good and the not-so-good.

Author Jack Canfield said, "If you want to be successful, you have to take 100% responsibility for everything that you experience in your life. This includes the level of your achievements, the results you produce, the quality of your relationships, the state of your health and physical fitness, your income, your debts, your feelings — everything!"

Then he added, "This is not easy."

And he continued, "In fact, most of us have been conditioned to blame something outside of ourselves for the parts of our life we don't like. We blame our parents, our bosses, our friends, our co-workers, our clients, our spouse, the weather, the economy, our astrological chart, our lack of money — anyone or anything we can pin the blame on. We never want to look at where the real problem is – ourselves."

Use Negativity As Motivation!

One of the most disparaging comments I dealt with came when an ex-husband told me, "If you leave me, you will fail! You need me! You'll never make more than $25,000."

He then said a few negative things about my face and body that were very unkind and hurtful. Then he added, "You'll come crawling back to me, and I won't take you back!"

Because those words came from someone I had loved and once respected, I could've taken that as gospel and accepted those words. I could have stayed in the relationship out of fear.

But I looked at it another way. I saw it as I had been given my marching orders. Those negative words were the most empowering words that I had ever heard, and they still echo in my mind to this day.

It was a defining moment for me and I had to choose which

path to take. What if I had stayed? How would my life be different today?

I'm so glad that I had the strength to leave. I went to some group classes at the Abuse Counseling Treatment Center and quickly discovered that I was in the best position of all. There were women at the meetings that still lived in fear. Others were living in the shelter because they had no way to take care of themselves. Some were bruised and battered.

I started helping some of those ladies. That was my best therapy. I felt so blessed. I also had perspective. No matter how hard you have it, just look around and you'll see so many more that are far worse off than you are.

One of my favorite quotes is from Dr. Wayne Dyer, who said, "I believe if you change the way you look at things, the things you look at change."

Through hard work, good business sense and timing, I became successful; and in January 2018, Gulfshore Life interviewed me about how I made my first million. Talking about mentors Jim and Ellie Newton, I said, "They taught me a lot about honesty and that when you give somebody your word, your word is more important than having a signed contract."

In persisting through other challenges, I've found ways to grow and succeed.

As a single parent, I went to school to learn the restaurant business. I knew the hospitality part, but I had no clue about running and operating a restaurant, nor the accounting that is required to make it successful and profitable.

I've sold, bought and built many businesses — and rebuilt many after hurricanes while looking at other opportunities in other communities.

I needed these adversities to get where I am. It's almost like God saying: So you don't like conflict, Sandy? Here's another dose of it. You can handle it.

Every obstacle prepared me to face each new challenge head on. When you are the leader in an organization, your staff need to be able to look to you for direction and motivation. The best things that have happened to me often have come from the worst situations. A good entrepreneur has grit and fortitude, hard work and perseverance.

It doesn't matter what your position is, you can be a leader. If you want to succeed, you need to be pleasant, knowledgeable, upbeat, well-groomed and motivated. Be a problem solver, not a complainer. Do your homework and learn the business. Come to work, ready to work. Be honest. Be part of the solution, not part of the problem. That's how you succeed.

As a good leader, you need to manage your time well and that means that you can't do it all. You need to empower others to do their job. Setting up an organization is fun and it takes skill. You lead from the top. You manage the managers and hold them accountable. You need to monitor them and set clear measurable goals. You need to motivate them and boost energy! Be tough on issues and not on people. Listen, ask and praise.

Dealing With Issues

I've learned to choose my battles wisely. Everything can't be personal. People will not only tire of you, but you'll cease being effective as well.

So be selective in what issues you want to pursue.

Susan Del Gatto once said this about procrastination: "If you choose to not deal with an issue, then you give up your right of control over the issue and it will select the path of least resistance."

And a few more wise words from Dr. Wayne Dyer, who said, "Our lives are a sum total of the choices we have made."

I haven't allowed others to get me down, because I've relied on God, family, good friends and a support system to get me through.

Your mindset in life is what matters most.

Automobile pioneer Henry Ford knew this as he once said, "Whether you think you can or you think you can't – you're right."

Throughout my life I've leaned on my support system to make the right choice on key decisions. I didn't decide based on what could make me the most money or would feed my ego. I often chose based on what needed to be done.

You know, reputation and character make a unique coupling.

There's the saying that reputation is what others think of us, while character is who we truly are.

I'll close with these profound words from Thomas Paine, who said, "Reputation is what men and women think of us; character is what God and angels know of us."

Entrepreneurial Mindset Q&A:

How did you respond when hit by adversity?

Did you keep your adversity inside or was it better when you shared your feelings?

Have you had the strength to help others when you were down?

How have you tried to motivate another person?

How are you at taking personal responsibility for all aspects of your life?

Do you make excuses for bad things that happen to you or do you take full responsibility?

Can you think of a time when you walked away from a situation and chose not to get involved?

CHAPTER 10

Life By The Water

"Mother, mother ocean,
I have heard you call
Wanted to sail upon your waters
since I was three feet tall
You've seen it all,
you've seen it all."

— Jimmy Buffett, "A Pirate Looks At Forty"

Do you have a favorite hobby? Or a way to unwind and get away from day-to-day stress?

My recreation is being on the water. Give me a lake, river or ocean and a boat and I'm a happy girl!

Among my early jobs as a youth included being a dishwasher for my Uncle Kelly and Aunt Jane at their Tradewinds Café.

I loved it!

I earned $5 a day and that was my water skiing money.

I saved half and spent half. When my day finished, I'd go home with my aunt and uncle, then change into my swimsuit. I had a friend waiting with her boat and we would water ski. I bought the gas and she had the boat!

I treasured those times.

Why?

It was here I fell in love with independence. I have been boating since I was a little girl.

Water is in my blood. I was raised in boating when I was a little girl.

My parents took their cabin cruiser from Chicago, and traveled down the Mississippi River to Cape Coral, Florida in the summer of 1959.

I believe if they didn't have two girls, my parents may have liked to live on the boat in Southwest Florida. As it was, the home they rented when they first lived in Cape Coral was walking distance from the yacht basin.

Boating time is family time. Some of my best weekends and vacations have been spent on the water with family and friends. My mom opened a little bait shop at the yacht basin and my sister and I would play around the docks while my mom sold bait and tackle to the fishermen. She did that to help pay the house rent and put gas in the car and boat.

There were no schools in Cape Coral and it was way before the Cape Coral bridges were built. We needed to drive through North Fort Myers to get to the bridge on U.S. 41 to go to Fort Myers.

Every time I went by Sanibel and Captiva islands as a youth boating, I found it charming. While I enjoyed that it was sparsely populated, what I really liked was the nature. There's so much preservation. People would chip in and buy parceled land to take it off the market and allow more preservation. Thanks to the Sanibel Captiva Conservation Foundation, more than 2,100 acres of land have been conserved and 1,500 square miles of water are monitored

This is Little Shell Island. It had a restaurant on it while I was growing up that my family frequented while boating. We became friends with the owners. Now, it has eroded to a tiny island on the right in the slow zone while leaving the Caloosahatchee River heading for the Sanibel Causeway or the miserable mile, steering toward Captiva Island along the intercoastal waterway.

while this acreage has created room for more than 700 turtle nests and 30 shorebird species.

We used to race sailboats in that area. There's competition, there's strategy and there are long-time friendships from those races.

The homes I've bought have been either right next to the Gulf of Mexico or minutes away.

The hotels I ran were on the beach or near it.

You can hear the tides or smell the salt air off the Gulf from some of the restaurants that I own on Captiva Island.

Two of my restaurants share the same name: Key Lime Bistro. One is on Captiva Island and the other is in Boca Grande on Gasparilla Island. Our next location will open inside Southwest Florida International Airport.

So it shouldn't surprise you that one of the properties I was interested in buying was an island.

Water's Dichotomy

Life on the water is incredibly ironic.

I've seen the best of times being by or on the water – and the worst.

Hurricanes have caused billions of dollars of damage to beaches and caused death and so much devastation to dear friends' lives and businesses.

Living on the water has its challenges. With my parents, we went through Hurricane Donna in Cape Coral in 1960. It was always considered the worst hurricane ever. We lost the roof off our home and all of our belongings from the storm's fury. And what wasn't lost from the storm was later lost by looters rummaging through our home.

We had a nice break of 40-plus years before the hurricanes started coming back.

In 2022 when Hurricane Ian came through, my husband, Tim and I watched TV intently. My parents had a home right on the back bay on Fort Myers Beach. It was about 45 years old and had wood-frame construction. They were supposed to come to our home, but Mom was delaying. In past hurricanes my parents would evacuate, but then they'd have to wait weeks before being allowed back in.

By 11 p.m., the night before Hurricane Ian was due to come, my parents were still at their home. When I called, they said they would come in the morning.

In the middle of the night, we received a call from Tim's daughter, Trista Kragh, who was in Naples. She said that Naples was already starting to flood and we better be prepared.

We were glued to the TV and couldn't sleep. Finally, about 3:30 a.m., we drove to their house. I called along the way and said that we were coming to pick them up.

By that time the rain was coming down in sheets and the roads had standing water. However, where my parents live, their street floods on heavy rain days.

At approximately 4:15 a.m., we loaded up their car and my husband drove it with my dad as a passenger. I drove our car with my mom. She wasn't happy with me because she was rushed.

I apologized and said that we got this call from Trista and that Hurricane Ian is coming our way. The water rose as we drove, but we returned to our home safely.

As we watched TV, we saw the sheriff's substation floating down Estero Boulevard. We saw devastation. We watched as NBC's Kellie Burns spoke with somebody that she knew in Boardwalk Caper Condos. They were totally flooded and desperately seeking advice as to what to do.

My parent's home was about one-eighth of a mile from there. We knew it was bad. Our insistence on taking my parents out of their Fort Myers Beach home and bringing them to our home during Hurricane Ian saved their lives. The house was totally destroyed.

With my parents being 88 and 92 at the time of that storm, their chances of surviving were next to none. God watched over them and helped alert us to pick them up.

Isn't it fascinating that the oceans and Gulf – where people will come from hundreds and thousands of miles away for peace, relaxation and tranquility – can be places of violence and destruction when visited by a powerful storm?

It's a union I've come to terms with. You're in a love-hate relationship with Mother Nature.

If you want to own a hotel or restaurant on the beach or in the tropics, is this something you're prepared to deal with?

Even if your business venture isn't near the water, all

entrepreneurs need to be prepared for the unexpected. And possessing a willingness to improvise and adapt to unforeseen events is critical for long-term success.

For me, life by the water has had its ebbs and flows for sure, but I can say without reservation that my numerous joyful moments on the water have far outweighed the sad ones.

Entrepreneurial Mindset Q&A:

What do you think about life on the water?

What activities do you enjoy most?

What do you do when you need a break?

What do you enjoy doing with family and friends?

Would you be willing to make a trade of being on the water while facing threats of a hurricane or even destruction?

Can you build a business around what you love to do for leisure and what brings you happiness?

CHAPTER 11

A Sister's Gift

"When you trust in God, you surrender your worries and fears to Him, knowing that He is in control. This act of surrender allows you to experience a deep sense of peace that surpasses human understanding. It is a peace that brings comfort, reassurance, and a steadfast hope."

– Spiritualthinking.com

My sister Beverly Chesnut and I are close, but we had our moments, especially as teens.

When our motel became our home, she didn't like it. We had to share a room.

Money was tight and my parents didn't have the cash to buy her a car. I bought her a Sunbeam Alpine convertible, but she had to drive me around. She really wasn't very happy having to haul around her little sister like a chauffeur! She barely tolerated me.

I was neat, she was not. When she left the motel, she was a true head turner! But the stack of tried-on clothes she left behind almost tripped me. So, you get the drift!

But just a few years later, I went to church with Beverly and her husband Steve. They got married fresh out of high school.

I quickly noticed she had become this different person. Like night and day.

It was a good difference. Really good.

She just had this way about her. She smiled and radiated peace and kindness. As I watched this transformation, a prevailing thought went through my mind:

Whatever she has, I want it.

So, when she invited me to attend her church, I jumped at the opportunity. I was 17.

Soon, Beverly and I continued to attend church as well as Bible study. She had given her life to Christ, and I soon followed.

Giving Your Life To Christ

So, what does that mean to give your life to Christ? For me, it was a life-changing experience.

That protective bubble I told you about remained as a defense mechanism. Inside that bubble was a mixed-up young lady who really didn't know how to trust anybody, especially a man.

I had an inner dread and when I looked in the mirror, I saw a fake. I was trying to smile my way through life and work hard for praise, but I didn't like myself. I thought the only way to get to God was by doing good things. Yet I knew that He saw through my facade.

That day, Pastor Jim Holbrook said that believing in God was not enough. He quoted James 2:19: You believe that God is one; you do well. Even the demons believe — and shudder!

There was never a time that I didn't believe in God or in Jesus, but I knew that something else was needed. That something else was knowing that no matter how hard we tried to be good, we could never earn our way into heaven. My mindset always thought that I had to do good deeds to get into heaven. I suddenly realized that it had nothing to do with that. I thought that I needed to be perfect. Of course, I wasn't perfect but rather than admit my mistakes, I would hide or cover them up. That caused dread or shame or feelings of self-doubt and insecurity.

That day, our pastor said that God knew everything about me and loved me just the way I was. It was a free gift and all that I needed to do was confess my wrongdoings and receive God's gift of forgiveness and ask Him into our lives.

Easter Sunday, 1974. That day changed my life.

It happened so quickly and freely. God transformed this insecure young lady into somebody who felt valued, loved, forgiven and worthy. Unconditionally.

No person could do it, but God. I now had a part of Him living in me. I now had strength to do anything. No matter what happened to me I knew that it would be okay because God had a plan for me. I knew that if I went down a wrong road, He would set me straight and that there must have been a reason for making that wrong turn.

Yes, it's the lessons learned. What a sense of peace that was! It revolutionized my life.

Life Is Good

Today, my beautiful sister has two degrees and is a minister and marriage and family counselor at McGregor Baptist. She's been married to Steve since 1972 and they have four children.

One of their sons, Steven, is a minister in Texas. Their

daughter, Krista, is a success in the insurance industry. Jonathan is a Cape Coral police officer, and their youngest son, Corban, is an entrepreneur and has a pizza restaurant on Captiva Island.

Through my openness to learn and grow and my sister's love, I have received the gift of faith. It's not really being religious, but it's a spirituality and a daily walk with God.

We regularly went to church, so I always believed. Suddenly, a light bulb went off at a time in my life when I wanted, needed and was willing to understand.

When I realized that God loved me just the way I was, that proved to be all

My beautiful sister Beverly, who continues to inspire me every day through her actions.

the difference. All I needed to do was recognize Him as my savior and invite Him to take over control of my life.

It was life-changing.

I suddenly realized and identified what transformed my sister. I also became a new person.

I never push my faith on other people, but they know they can come to me when they want advice or somebody to pray for them.

Unwavering Faith

Through all my adversities in life, I've never lost faith. I didn't know how or what, but I always knew something better was ahead as Jim Newton wrote to me.

I also felt a light guiding me. I have never felt alone. He is with me.

Because of that, I don't dwell on the past. I talk to God and I pray. I put one foot in front of the other and ask God for His will in my life. I ask Him to close the door before I walk through it if He wants to stop me. I asked Him to send a sign.

I must admit, sometimes God has sent huge signs in the way of obstacles. Because I'm a problem solver, sometimes I didn't know I hit a roadblock, so I ignored the sign! A perfect case of lessons learned!

Perhaps I've learned most after a wrong turn. In times when I've tripped and fallen, I've gotten back up bruised and a little sore, but every time I dusted off my behind and got back to it. That's grit.

The detours have led me to new friends, new businesses and new experiences. Yet, I value the lifelong friends and the business relationships that have spanned many decades.

Things do turn out better eventually. You simply must believe. I guess that's why they call it faith.

Entrepreneurial Mindset Q&A:

Do you consider yourself faith-based?

What role, if any, does faith play in your life?

What memories, if any, do you have of attending a religious service?

When you had a difficult decision to make, did you pray on it?

Would you like to speak to someone more about this topic?

CHAPTER 12

Leadership

"Above all, every morning, you need to take
a daily infusion of three key ingredients
for successful leadership. One is for
commitment, one is for courage
and one is for compassion."

- Merrily Dean Baker, former athletic director
at Michigan State and former interim AD
at Florida Gulf Coast University

In a journey that started in 1998 that took her on a cross-continental trip from Istanbul, Turkey to Naples, Florida, Florida Gulf Coast University President Dr. Aysegul Timur wanted to give 100 percent commitment and dedication to everything she did.

While learning English, she said she wanted to earn a PhD in the United States. She had a laser focus on that vision.

As an aide, teacher and instructor, she wanted to use technology and experiential learning to motivate students.

Now, as FGCU's leader, she wants to bring that same energy

and electricity.

"I always believed in one of my ways of describing a leader as a person who would influence," she said. "Leadership to me is being an influence on a vision where you want to take all others. As leading a team, you want others to believe in the mission and vision moving forward.

"It's collaboration but wanting every person to feel like they're a part of it and they want to help you get there. It's not just, 'Hey, we're at a table, let's do this.' Everyone provides input, everyone has buy in and they feel part of the process."

To achieve that goal, President Timur feels there are three P's that are essential.

> **Passion:** "It's very important that you care about what you do and that you believe in that and that it describes you," she said. "You don't just see it as a job. You feel you're making a difference. I'm passionate about higher education. It transformed me and I want to help it transform others.

> **Partnership:** "I don't think anything can get done without collaboration and inclusivity and working with people who have the same goals," she said.

> **Performance:** "When you combine passion and partnership you get performance and results. You have achieved something bigger than yourself. You can't do it by yourself. As a leader, you have to influence people on that shared vision."

I love these principles Dr. Timur uses to guide herself and those she leads. Every strong leader will develop their own approach that fits their business or industry, but no matter who or where you lead, at the heart of exceptional leadership is honesty and humility.

Leading Early
During high school, I started to sell Avon products as part of a class project.

I'd say hi to everyone and ask if they'd buy Avon. I was not afraid to talk to strangers, although I didn't go around neighborhoods door-to-door selling products.

I helped customers with their purchases, made invoices and placed orders.

I didn't have a goal of winning a pink car. My Avon career didn't last long, but it helped me develop some core traits in bookkeeping. While this experience also helped me communicate with people of all ages, I also noticed my interactions with teachers were on more of a personal level.

By the end of the year, I received a number of awards, including Future Business Leader of America and Most Likely To Succeed.

As I started businesses at an early age, I learned how to work with people and motivate them. I wanted those who I employed to see me as someone who would help guide them on a successful path.

Years later, I still feel the same way.

What Is Leadership?
The dictionary definition of leadership is a person who guides or directs a group.

But it must be more than that.

I think leadership is being able to successfully gather a group of people and help guide them in the same direction you're heading.

After all, leaders lead.

There are many types of leaders. They aren't just in political arenas, boardrooms or restaurants.

Top-performing athletes are seen as leaders not just because of their abilities, but also for how they motivate their teammates to achieve their best.

High school and college students who help run various organizations are seen as leaders, especially when their efforts make money for the group. Solo singers and top musicians who are front men – and women - for bands also are praised for their leadership.

In a speech I once gave, I said being a good leader involves a combination of skills, actions and personal attributes. Those include integrity, vision, accountability, empathy, communication, inspiration, decisive decision making, delegation, flexibility/adaptability, resiliency, gratitude, and even being able to respectfully deal with complaints.

Here's an expanded definition of these key attributes:

Integrity: Show you are genuine by being honest and transparent. Personal ethics builds trust.

Vision: Be clear on where you want to go and share that vision effectively with the team.

Empathy: Tell people that what they're offering is a valuable service. Understanding their needs, concerns, feelings and perspectives helps you connect with them and creates a supportive environment.

Communication: Communicating isn't just talking but listening. When I speak and convey my thoughts, I'm succinct and clear, which helps all understand. When listening, I take notes at staff meetings. Before the next meeting, I want to hear from each individual. Then, an action plan is created.

Inspiration: Through empathy and communication, I help foster an environment of creativity, acceptance and value. When a team member is valued, it answers the why questions: Why am I here? Why do I devote so much time to this organization? Why is what we do so important? When a team member can answer those questions positively, their productivity should grow because they're inspired.

Delegation: Effective leaders recognize they need help. Trust your team members. Assign duties and tasks and let them know they need to follow up with results. Then hold them accountable. I always assign tasks on an individual's strengths and I empower them to take ownership of their work. We use a personality profile in my leadership team so not all the strengths are in one area.

Flexibility/Adaptability: Good leaders adjust the plan and strategy. There always will be challenges in a changing environment. During COVID-19, the word 'pivot' became our mantra. Nothing stayed the same, nothing was status quo, especially in the hospitality and restaurant industry. Challenges often came daily after mandates from the President or governor. We adjusted strategies in response to those challenges. We had a similar approach to Hurricanes Ian, Helene and Milton.

Resiliency: Obstacles and setbacks are constant. A resilient leader maintains focus and perseverance and demonstrates a positive attitude in the face of adversity. Everybody is looking at you to lead the way. Sometimes, when I felt like I couldn't do it anymore, I realized that I had to be there and do it.

Gratitude: A spirit of gratefulness creates a culture of others also being grateful. If I can't say something nice or uplifting, I don't unless it's truly important. I thank my staff, my customers and my suppliers. Even after hurricanes, I'm more grateful. I take nothing for granted. My takeaway is that God makes us better in adversity. By exhibiting and embodying traits of gratitude, a leader can successfully guide their team toward effectiveness and success. By showing a "Can-do" attitude, I'm driven toward solutions, not dwelling on problems.

Complaints: I would rather learn of an issue rather than a bad review. Good leaders want to know of problems because if they don't know, how can they fix them? My staff also needs to know how to effectively handle a complaint and bring it to a manager. Look for a solution so the complaint doesn't happen again. Great customer service must be paramount. It should be part of your culture and environment. There's nothing wrong with being imperfect. I learned it's better to drop the ego than break a relationship. Ego can keep one aloof. With friendships, you're never alone.

In my 20s, I took on my greatest leadership challenge of all – being a mother. Ladies, never underestimate the importance of motherhood.

You learn early with children you not only have to feed and clothe them, but you also have to communicate with them in a way they understand.

You can't let them do anything they want, but you are there to lend your support and encourage them to grow and be responsible.

Being a mother is the greatest joy of my life, and I also have the added bonus of being a grandmother.

Admit When You're Wrong

My dad once told me everyone makes mistakes. He said, "That's why they put erasers on the end of pencils."

It's a lesson I've carried with me.

A few years ago, one of my restaurants had a catering job, which included 100 appetizers. I forgot to follow through on it.

When an email came and the customer asked to pick up the appetizers, I took responsibility and offered to pick up the items myself.

More studies are showing that people have more respect when leaders admit mistakes.

In a March 2024 article for Forbes, Dr. Nicole Lipkin, who writes about the psychology of work and leadership, shared that the ability to admit being wrong transforms good leaders into great ones.

"Contrary to the traditional notion of leadership often associated with unwavering confidence and infallibility, acknowledging one's mistakes fosters a culture of humility, learning, and adaptability within an organization," Dr. Lipkin wrote.

She also quoted Carol Dweck, who wrote the book, Mindset. In it, she talks about fixed and growth mindsets.

Dweck wrote:

> A fixed mindset is one who believes that their abilities, intelligence, and talent are fixed. Any success or failure an individual with a fixed mindset receives in life will be an affirmation of their ever-static abilities.
>
> Thus, to maintain an unblemished self-image, the fixed mindsets don't typically put themselves into a situation where they might fail.
>
> A growth mindset is the belief that we can always develop our abilities further. The growth mindsets don't view failure as a confirmation of their immutable abilities, but rather opportunities to learn and grow from the experience.
>
> Thus, the growth mindsets don't shy away from experiences where they may not succeed because it's all part of their self-development continuum.

Working with researcher Karina Schumann, Dweck's study sought to answer the question: Does having a fixed or growth mindset matter when it comes to admitting fault? Their research said yes.

> When it comes to accepting responsibility, the growth mindsets of the world, "feel less threatened by accepting responsibility because they are more likely to view the situation as an opportunity for them to grow as a person and develop their relationship with the victim."

Conversely, what are the potential consequences of a leader not admitting wrongdoing? Lipkin wrote that this can lead to employees having a loss in:

- Productivity
- Morale
- Innovation
- Psychological Safety
- Meaning In The Workplace
- Loyalty

The Bright Lights

It doesn't matter what your position is, you can be a leader. If you want to succeed, you need to be human as well as pleasant, knowledgeable, upbeat, well-groomed and motivated.

Humans make mistakes, so choose to be a problem solver and not a complainer.

Do your homework and learn the business. Come to work ready to work. Be honest and be part of the solution – not part of the problem. That's how you succeed.

And when you're the leader in an organization, the bright lights shine the brightest. The pressure is on. Your staff needs to be able to look to you for direction and motivation.

A good leader excels at time management. That means you can't do it all. You need to empower others to do their jobs, give them responsibility and trust they'll do the job. Setting up an organization is fun but it takes skill.

You lead from the top. You manage the managers and hold them accountable. You need to monitor them and set measurable goals. You need to motivate them and boost energy!

Be tough on issues, not on people. Listen, ask and praise.

Entrepreneurial Mindset Q&A:

What is your definition of leadership?

Can you share examples of when you were a leader?

What did you learn from being a leader? Is that something you enjoyed?

Do you see yourself being a leader in your profession? What will you need to achieve that?

Do you remember an example of a time you put your ego aside?

Do you remember avoiding saying something negative, which became the right decision?

CHAPTER 13

Running A Restaurant

"If anything is good for pounding
humility into you permanently,
it's the restaurant business."

- The late Anthony Bourdain,
chef and TV personality

Do you want to run a restaurant?

Do you know how hard it is?

Are you looking for the ultimate challenge?

The success rate, or rather, the non-success rate of restaurants, is eye-opening. Maybe even discouraging.

According to The National Restaurant Association, 60 percent of restaurants go out of business after one year.

After five years, the percentage rises to 80 percent.

While being in that 20 percent is a good feeling, I do have one experience where I fell among the 80 percent. I'll get into that more later.

I do have empathy for people who go into this business and don't succeed. It doesn't matter if it's a food truck or five-star establishment, there's so many challenges.

I never thought I'd own a restaurant after working for my Uncle Kelly; and years after buying my first restaurant and taking a summer course at Cornell University, the work hasn't gotten any easier.

Having such debilitating events like COVID-19, red tide and hurricanes really humbled me. It also wiped out many restaurateurs.

But as José Andrés, chef and founder of World Central Kitchen said, "The business of feeding people is the most amazing business in the world."

At Keylime Bistro, my first restaurant, where I learned so many valuable lessons on my path as a restaurant owner.

Philip Rosenthal, television writer and producer, added, "A good restaurant is like a vacation; it transports you, and it becomes a lot more than just about the food."

From owning restaurants on Captiva Island and in Boca Grande on Gasparilla Island, we're able to create a family-friendly, beach-getaway vibe.

We play a variety of music, based on the venue.

At RC Otter's Island Eats, we play island tunes.

At our Mexican restaurant, Cantina Captiva, we play island surf tunes, Latino music and reggae, particularly Bob Marley.

Jazz, Spanish guitar and a variety of music are featured at Key Lime Bistro.

For fine dining at Sunshine Seafood Café & Wine Bar, we'll play quiet dinner music like Frank Sinatra and more modern dinner music.

Each individual restaurant has its own character.

But having a successful restaurant goes beyond creating the right vibe and having the right music. A person buying a restaurant must know everything that goes into running it or have a partner who is knowledgeable in areas where you are not.

Here is a list of the most important characteristics a restaurateur must have:

You need to lead: Part of leadership comes from leading by example, whether that means picking up trash in the parking lot, working nights and weekends or being the first person to arrive after a problem. When Keylime Bistro flooded, we put on sea boots and brought the squeegees. With our sons helping, we had a bucket brigade and pushed the water out. We did it together. Sometimes, you can't be too proud of getting your hands dirty or getting a few blisters.

Market your restaurant: Don't expect to open your doors and patrons to just walk in. Whether it be signs, social media, traditional advertising or getting involved in the community, you must get the word out.

Work long, hard, untraditional hours: There are times you will feel like the restaurant owns you. Many restaurants are open more than eight hours a day as well as holidays and weekends.

Hire problem solvers: I try to hire people on my team and empower them to work hard, take on challenges and come up with solutions rather than complain and say, "I can't do that." That makes me lose confidence and question if they're really in it for the right reasons. Because I expect more, I pay more.

Hire a flexible chef: Your chef can't just make wonderful entrees. Your chef also must be reliable and open to change.

Hire a good restaurant manager: That person needs to be able to put out a lot of fires or potential fires. It's not just about pleasing the customer, it's about knowing what to do when your chef yells at servers and they lose their mojo.

Be on the lookout for future talent: Look at raising your leaders from within your organization because they know your culture and they fit into that culture.

Take care of your employees: This can be done in several ways. If your employees are traveling 30-40 minutes, try to schedule them so they'll be busy on their shifts. When we had to close because of COVID-19 and hurricanes, we had our employees come in and help us remodel and do some maintenance. We later were able to do deliveries and take food orders. I lost out on the Paycheck Protection Program (PPP) money for six weeks of payroll because the government didn't make it retroactive, but there was a grant program for every employee rehired so I did the right thing.

Listen to your staff but don't be a doormat: I have a chain of command, but there's also an open-door policy if there are legitimate problems with employees and managers. Personality issues may arise. Employees need to know there is a difference

At Captiva's Keylime Bistro. I plan to open another Keylime Bistro in Southwest Florida International Airport in 2025.

between serious issues and issues they should be able to work out. This goes back to taking on challenges and coming up with solutions.

Keep accurate books: There's payroll, there's invoices on deliveries and there are customers' receipts. If you're on top of your bookkeeping, you can see when something's not right, even if customers are paying in cash. Look at bank statements closely. Match your customers' receipts with what's being deposited. Are employees putting all deposits in the bank? Is there food missing? There can be variations, but when you drill down and things are not fitting into the percentages they should, then you immediately know there is a problem that needs to be addressed.

Make tough decisions: When I had strong suspicions and came to the conclusion all the staff members were either taking from the till or not being forthcoming, I shut that business down. Nipped it in the bud. Not only were the food-cost percentages out of line, but so were the liquor-cost percentages and labor-cost percentages. The physical-plant costs were normal. That points to one thing: money not accounted for. I didn't tell anybody until I went in and said, "Everyone is out." I gave them two week's pay and I changed the locks. I cleaned house and I closed the restaurant. My suspicions were right. When those actions happen, there can be no second chances. Trust has been broken and it can't be repaired.

Know what inventory you need – and what you don't: Trying to anticipate what your customers want can be like trying to herd cats. It's nearly impossible. That's why we often prep after people order as opposed to pre-prep. But where you can help yourself is charting what people order. If you offer a special and there are 100 orders, that gives you an idea how popular some items are. Also, if your waitress or waiter shares that today's grouper is a fresh catch, that also can help. Watching inventory became much more important after the pandemic as prices went up more than 10 percent. There's also a gas surcharge. As a result, some menu items went up.

Be active in the community: Being part of organizations in your community is important. Donating food or gift cards to causes or fundraisers often helps. However, you can't give to all causes. Though paying it forward has its benefits as I'm finding residents often support those restaurants that support their schools, churches and events.

Work with other restaurants: Not everyone is going to eat in your restaurant every single night. They may eat at your competitor's. Over the course of the winter season, I believe there's enough customers for everyone. If someone is looking for something that's not on your menu, why not suggest a competitor? Maybe they'll do the same for you. The restaurant owners on Sanibel and Captiva islands also have gotten together. There's a good group of 8-10 people. When we put our voices together, we convinced the county commissioners to waive tolls on six Sundays in the summer for our employees.

Persevere through major adversity: When Hurricane Ian hit us in September 2022, we had little time to feel sorry for ourselves. We hit the ground running. Since we didn't have the Sanibel bridge connecting us to Fort Myers for three weeks, we had two-to-four boats go out, which took workers and neighbors. We had to take the cottages down to their foundations while our restaurants were hit hard as well. The islanders joined together to preserve the island's history, which includes the Sanibel Lighthouse and the Sanibel Historical Museum and Village. These landmarks reopened in March 2023. That was exciting. We made lemonade out of really sour lemons.

Have your restaurant in a desirable area: That means having your restaurant in a community where you will be supported. That either means having residents who either have a disposable income and like to dine out or are regular patrons because, well, they have to eat and yours is the food they really like.

Menu balance: Most people like to try new offerings on the menu; but many like the same dishes every time they come in. Sometimes, some menu items have to go.

Know your customers: Customers can be wonderful in their praise. Appreciate that. Customers also can be critical. Respect that. Aim to be better. You can't improve if you don't know what the problems are. Customers also can be tricky. Anticipate that. Sometimes there are long waits during peak season.

Some customers will put in reservations at three different restaurants and when the first one calls, they are no-shows for the other reservations. For this reason, we offer online reservations. When they make reservations in person, customers have five minutes to respond when their name is called or someone else gets their table. And customers may be ugly. Be understanding of that – to a point. They may have had a bad day or they had problems while on vacation. Some people can be perpetually unhappy. It may have nothing to do with their order.

Make it fun: You don't have to be a five-star, Michelin-rated restaurant to give your patrons a great experience. Casual dress is welcomed at our restaurants and guests can leave their dogs on the patios. There often is live music with ring games and cut outs to take pictures. With weddings, people often request our snail trolley, which is a Jeep that has been converted into what looks like a snail. We call it our S Car Go. It has a trolley behind it to transport people from South Seas Resort to the village. It always brings a smile to people; and children like to take rides. I never realized in creating the S Car Go trolley that brides and grooms would like to take a ride as well. It adds a whimsical touch to our island of Captiva. We are family oriented and golf-cart friendly.

I do not think everyone is cut out to be in the restaurant business. Many have this dream of owning a restaurant and that it can be so much fun. They romanticize that it's lovely being a host, and you meet interesting people. They envision everyone who comes in is appreciative, loves the food and atmosphere and everything is wonderful.

That often happens. When it does, it is the best business in the world.

But there is that saying that 10 percent of people can cause 90 percent of your problems. And we didn't even touch on if a person over drinks.

Combine that with the hours, the bills, the staff and increasing food prices. The restaurant business also can leave you awake at night.

When that happens, get up and do some bookkeeping.

Then go to bed, get up later in the morning and drive to your restaurant with a smile on your face.

It's a new day.

Keylime Bistro on a sunny day on Captiva Island.

Entrepreneurial Mindset Q&A:

_____

Have you ever thought of owning a restaurant?

Why would you want to own a restaurant?

Do the statistics from The National Restaurant Association discourage you or make you more determined?

How many of the above skills are you good at? What skills do you need to work at?

How do you feel about working nights, weekends and holidays?

CHAPTER 14

Shared Vision

---

*"Look for three things in a person:
intelligence, energy and integrity.
If they don't have the last one,
don't even bother with the first two."*

— Warren Buffett

When I started my cleaning business, we built it to the point where we needed employees. Reliable employees.

I hired students who I had been with in Bible study or our youth group. I trusted them. Since we worked at night and nobody was in the offices we cleaned, I needed to know they wouldn't take pens or notepads off desks.

No matter whether it was the first business I had or the current businesses I operate, working with honest, hard-working and dedicated people is crucial. And it's important at every level. From someone who you just hired to someone you went into business with, building trust with your team is vital.

When relationships don't work or business opportunities come up, difficult decisions need to be made. And each of these choices can be defining moments in a person's life.

They were defining for me, even though I was barely out of high school.

At age 20, I ended a marriage/business partnership. Because of a variety of factors personally and professionally, I came to a quick conclusion it was time to move on.

When you have a partner in a business or a partner in life, it helps tremendously if you have a similar commitment and that you're evenly yoked. That means the same ethics, same values, same morals, same work ethic and same vision, both short- and long-term.

The moral of the story: Choose your partners wisely. Don't just jump into a business opportunity with someone. Do your research. Sit down with that person, ask tough questions and try to gauge whether that person is as committed as you are.

My high school senior class picture at age 17, long before I met Jim Newton, and he shared his advice with me that, "The best is yet to be." There is so much promise in tomorrow!

Fortunately, I learned this hard lesson before I had children. After the marriage ended, we divided our assets and sold our home. The cash I made on the home sale helped me move forward.

I took solace in the fact that owning a cleaning business wasn't my long-range goal. Owning a hotel was.

I also was young enough to bounce back, which I did rather quickly.

Clear Goals

Before getting into a partnership, my own goals, beliefs and ethics have to be crystal clear.

One of the most important lessons I learned was to rely on God, good friends and a support system to help me make the right choices on important decisions in my life. I encourage everyone to build a strong, trusted team of confidants you can use as a sounding board. My personal ethics start with how I do my paperwork.

My mother helped me with my first payroll. She taught me how to balance the books rather than hiring a bookkeeping service. This saved me money, but also provided me with a strong foundation for all future businesses.

As a bookkeeper, one has a choice of reporting every dime or pocketing some. Taking shortcuts in the short term can hurt you in the long term. For example, if you sell a business, its value is based on the company's profits. So if you don't include transactions paid in cash to avoid paying extra taxes, you hurt yourself in the long run. When reported profit margins are less, it'll prevent you from assessing your business for its maximum value when you sell it.

Having integrity in how you handle your bookkeeping is very important in building your company – and your reputation. Not only is it the right thing to do, but it'll be a lot easier to sleep at night with a clear conscience.

The Right Business Partner

Once your goals, beliefs and ethics are clear, it's key to have a business partner with whom you can make joint decisions that can benefit both of you in the long term. These decisions can potentially set you up for many years.

When I was college age, instead of going to college, I helped remodel and work at my new hotel called The Sandcastle

Island Resort, just blocks from my parents' hotel.

It was a dream come true. My business partner Bob – who also was my husband – lived on site in a home that overlooked the lagoon. It gave us privacy and soon after, we started remodeling it because we were married and wanted to start a family.

It was a happy and simple time. We didn't need two cars so we sold my car. My husband did the maintenance while I worked the front desk. In our free time, we competitively raced sailboats.

In 1979, I met a man named Keith Trowbridge, who made an offer on our hotel. We agreed to sell and made a good profit.

Our realtor was James D. Newton. The start of a beautiful relationship, as Humphrey Bogart said.

Keith Trowbridge had started buying waterfront hotels and motels all along the coastline. He turned these into what we now call timeshares and interval ownerships.

Keith had started to establish himself as a timeshare guru.

Jim and Ellie Newton as I remembered them back when we were business partners.

In a story written by his public relations chief, Marge Lennon, Trowbridge sold his Captran properties 'by the slice' in 1974 with a logo that resembled a pie-shaped slice of a pizza. He had developed the 31-unit Sanibel Beach Club, recognized as the first purpose-built timeshare resort in North America on exclusive Sanibel Island.

There had been around 45 conversion resorts, but this was the first building designed and built specifically for the purpose of use as a timeshare resort. The resort was sold out in 18 months. A marble and bronze plaque remains on the property today to indicate this distinction.

Keith was a brilliant man who told the media and owners about every aspect of how this new real estate technique worked. Keith also authored the first book on timesharing, published by Simon & Schuster in 1981. It sold 50,000 copies. They always called him "The Father of Timeshare."

Keith and his wife Doris were friends of mine until his passing in 2021. Keith always joked that he started me on my road to success. To be honest, my ex-husband Bob and I shared in those profits from selling that hotel, but it was a big step forward.

And with any large business transaction, as we did then, it's always important to remember the tax man is right around the corner.

Entrepreneurial Mindset Q&A:

What life-defining moment have you had?

Was it a college choice, relationship choice, professional choice, job choice or all four?

How did you make your decision?

Did you consult anybody before making your decision?

Did you find your first instinct proved to be best? Or did you find extensive analysis worked well?

CHAPTER 15

Uncommon Friends

"… I have written about them
as they revealed themselves to me."

— Jim Newton in sharing the lives of
Thomas Edison, Henry Ford,
Harvey Firestone, Alexis Carrel
and Charles Lindbergh in his
book *Uncommon Friends*

Do you have a mentor?

It's good to have one, maybe even a couple of mentors.

I think it helps if they are different ages as mentors of different ages will usually provide different perspectives.

Motivational speaker Jim Rohn once said, "You are the average of the five people you spend the most time with."

With that thought in mind, it's important to choose your friends wisely.

While I've learned so much from my contemporaries, I also have gleaned a lot of insights from those who are much older. They've lived life, they've had experiences.

People like Ellie and Jim Newton.

Jim is known for being the author of *Uncommon Friends*, a book on his unique friendships with Thomas Edison, Henry Ford, Harvey Firestone, Alexis Carrel and Charles Lindbergh.

Ironically, he also played a major role in finding Ann Morrow Lindbergh and Charles Lindbergh a place to stay on Captiva Island when they visited.

While on the island, Ann Morrow Lindberg picked up shells while walking on the beach for inspiration. She wrote about youth and age; love and marriage; peace, solitude and contentment.

The book, Gift from the Sea, has sold more than 3 million copies and has been translated into 45 languages.

Of all my memories of Jim, my most cherished was watching him and wife Ellie as they came to the church we attended. Ellie always snuggled next to Jim and read him the Sunday morning newspaper as he drove.

My great friends and mentors, Jim and Ellie Newton.

They didn't have bucket seats. They wanted a bench seat so she could be right next to him.

Often, they sped right by us, totally caught up in the moment. When they got out of the car, they walked into church hand-in-hand.

Ahhh, that's romance.

Ellie passed away at 104 in 2003, just four years after her Jimmy. They were married 56 years.

They made such an indelible mark and impact on my life during our friendship.

I'm sure you've heard of the expression, "What would God think?" While I use that, I often have asked myself, "What would Jim and Ellie think or do?"

His real estate company helped guide us as we sold the first hotel I owned.

Through his book Uncommon Friends, I met Walter Cronkite, Tom Brokaw, Anne Morrow Lindbergh, Charles Lindbergh, Jimmy Buffett and Silvia Eagle.

Ellie and Jim also taught me a lot about honesty. They said, "When you give somebody your word, the word is more important than having a signed contract."

Resorts, Rentals And Condos

After Jim helped us in the sale of SandCastle Island Resort, he asked for our help with his property management company. My former husband Bob and I also formed a property management company and we became partners.

The condominium boom was on.

Condos went up all along the coastlines. His company had so many clients, but he needed help in the management of the rentals and complexes.

As we quickly made an impression on him, Jim said, "If we're going to be partners, I want to hear your thoughts."

Ellie, who often was at Jim's side, would add, "What do you think, dear?"

That was a revelation. They brought me out of my shell. Our interactions with them gave me confidence, made me stretch myself and encouraged me to dream bigger.

There were 400 rentals and 13 condominium complexes that we handled. We bought several condos and rented them while we had several pre-construction contracts to buy more vacation rentals.

The simple life that we left in owning one hotel started getting very busy in managing all these properties, but things became even more challenging when interest rates rose.

From 1971 to 1981, rates went from 5.75% to 22.3%.

However, the property management company thrived.

Jim and I became partners for a few years and during that time, we developed a close friendship that lasted until he passed away.

Uncommon Friends, The Book

After agreeing to sell his real estate company, Jim went ahead with a friend's suggestion to write a book on his associations with Edison, Ford, Firestone, Carrel and Lindbergh.

It helped greatly that Jim meticulously kept a journal with noted times and places, key phrases and vivid impressions for 50 years.

"Knowing them did much to shape my life," Jim said while adding his observations. "Edison, who never gave up, but turned a thousand failures into triumph; Ford, with his imagination constantly grappling with new ideas; Firestone, who maintained a rocklike integrity amidst the shifting sands of business expediency; Carrel, who could lift you in a single conversation from the street to the stars; and

This photo captures the fellowship of these great men.
Seated, left to right, Henry Ford, Thomas Edison and
Harvey Firestone. Standing, left to right, unknown, Fred Ott,
assistant to Edison and the man in one of Edison's first films,
"The Sneeze," one of Firestone's sons and Jim Newton.

Lindbergh, never content to pursue one great purpose, but
constantly reaching for ever more challenging goals."

Uncommon Friends has received excellent reviews over
the years. A reviewer on Goodreads called it, "a delightful
portrayal of five great men who shared special friendships
and common visions." Another review called the book, "A
unique opportunity to share a view of the personal side of
some legendary historical figures."

Valuable Lesson
Uncommon Friends never would have been written if Jim
didn't have the ability at an early age to compromise.

Mina Edison and a group of local ladies wanted to have a

statue built of The Lady at the Well that would be a centerpiece for a subdivision called Edison Park that Jim helped oversee.

Before the statue was finished, some ladies sneaked in to take a look, only to see that the "lady" was naked.

They gasped at the sight of the statue.

The Fort Myers ladies were more conservative and they didn't want any part of a nude sculpture. Summoned to the Edison home, Jim listened as Mina shared her and the ladies' feelings.

Now Jim, who was in his 20s at the time and maybe more open-minded, could've been stubborn, dug in and ignored the women's concerns.

However, he offered a compromise of putting a veil on the "lady." The women agreed.

That led to Jim Newton having a treasured friendship with Mina and Thomas Edison as well as Henry Ford and Alexis Carrel and Charles Lindbergh and Anne Morrow Lindbergh and everyone in their circles.

The moral of the story: Choose your battles. It's as important to know which ones you can lose as much as those you can win.

Former Florida Everblades hockey coach Greg Poss agrees with this notion. He wrote a book about optimizing mental performance called Your Brain Deserves 10 Minutes Every Day. In the book, he asked the question, "Is it better to be right or powerful?"

I pass along Jim's lesson of compromise when I talk about Christian principles and ethics as a traveling speaker.

I share how important it is to be true to your word, to be ethical, to be honest and to be Godly, even if it costs you business deals.

I also share how God changed my life.

Uncommon Friends Offshoots

In 1993, Fran Myers and John Albion founded the Uncommon Friends Foundation. I soon joined the board of directors.

The mission was to carry on the generational values Jim Newton wrote about.

While volunteering at our church and children's school, I had an idea: Why not use lessons Jim shared in Uncommon Friends as a character curriculum for our children?

Working with the Lee County School district, we developed a curriculum for fourth-graders, then younger students, then older. We held a teacher's workshop where we taught the teachers. It was continuing education.

Besides learning of Edison's inventions – which included the incandescent light bulb, the phonograph and motion picture camera – students also received insights into solving problems, having persistence and dealing with adversity. Edison once said, "I have not failed. I've just found 10,000 ways that won't work."

Our classes had lessons in trust, ethics, being truthful, listening to another's viewpoint and sometimes, having social graces and agreeing to disagree.

Documentary

In 1999, John Biffar, who would go on to earn nine Emmy Awards, produced Uncommon Friends of the Twentieth Century. The PBS documentary premiered at Barbara B. Mann Theater and brought a lot of attention to Southwest Florida.

Former CBS Evening News anchorman Walter Cronkite narrated the documentary.

Celebrities who attended included Jimmy Buffett, Senator Connie Mack III, Anne Morrow Lindbergh and King Michael of Romania.

I still remember hearing Jimmy Buffett fly in on his personal seaplane, a Grumman HU-16 Albatross flying boat. That seaplane was a big part of Jimmy's book, A Pirate Looks at 50, one I read with great interest. He landed and docked the seaplane at the Sanibel Marriott Resort & Spa.

A few minutes later, Jimmy listened as Walter Cronkite and I shared sailing stories. He had a Westsail 43 with a canoe stern – the same sailboat I had. He later moved on to sail a Hinckley.

As I chatted with these two men, I had one of those pinch-me moments. Two of my idols were right in front of me and we were swapping stories.

Jim and Ellie invited friends from all over the world to the event. Some of those attending they had met through their long-time commitment to Moral Re-armament, an international moral and spiritual movement.

Developed by American minister Frank Buchman's Oxford group in 1938, the Christian-based movement grew into an informal international network of people of all faiths and backgrounds. It advocated 'The Four Absolutes' – absolute honesty; absolute purity; absolute unselfishness; and absolute love.

They held an international conference in Switzerland. One of the movement's core ideas was the belief that changing the world starts with seeking change.

Later, the organization's name changed to Initiatives of Change before dissolving in 2001.

John Biffar has kept the memories of Uncommon Friends alive with a documentary called Blown Away, The Spirit of Recovery.

Besides capturing stunning footage of Hurricane Ian's fury and the devastation it left behind, the documentary chronicled the caring and bravery displayed by today's Uncommon Friends, men and women who helped others in their darkest hours, showcasing the incredible resilience and compassion of community members in the face of disaster.

Erik Lindbergh, grandson of Charles Lindbergh, and I were among the many voices in the documentary, which also played homage to Thomas Edison, Henry Ford and James Newton.

In May 2024, Blown Away won first place in the Best Documentary category at the Greater Fort Myers Film Festival.

Entrepreneurial Mindset Q&A:

Do you have a mentor?

If you do, how has that person influenced your life?

What kind of questions do you ask your mentor?

How long do you think you'll continue communicating with your mentor?

CHAPTER 16

Captiva's Charm

---

*"The beach is not the place to work;
to read, write or think."*

— Anne Morrow Lindbergh
while on Captiva Island

Few people have the chance to work where they play.

I do. I've turned my youthful joy of boating and sailing around Sanibel and Captiva islands off the coast of Florida into a profession of providing visitors and customers wonderful experiences through the restaurants and properties I own in Boca Grande on Gasparilla Island and on Captiva Island.

And now, I feel a duty to help renovate and preserve an area, a destination, a style of life that brings people here from all over the world. There are quite a few celebrities who visit or spend a good part of their winters on the islands, but their privacy is always respected.

I have to admit, I chuckled a bit when I had a story written on me via artificial intelligence. It referred to me as a woman that offered, "Change on the horizon. ... A woman with an unyielding vision and indomitable spirit." It said I was, "Synonymous with transformation." It said that I, "Preserved properties historically," and that I, "Keep the historic village intact." Those descriptors made me feel like the new sheriff in town, a heroine.

Truth is, I'm quite proud of helping Captiva Island retain its charm despite commercial development, hurricanes, the BP Oil Spill, COVID-19, blue-green algae and red tide.

That's what entrepreneurs do. They help enterprises dear to them and do what they can through rough times as well as prosperity.

I felt such joy to see Captiva Island packed with customers for the Island Hopper Songwriter Fest in the fall of 2023, almost a year to the day after Hurricane Ian hit in September 2022.

People listened to great music, sampled our local cuisine and saw how we're recovering from the costliest storm in Florida's history.

My fellow restaurateurs didn't want to have the event unless Key Lime Bistro was part of it.

So we opened – sort of.

The front-deck servers welcomed customers, but the rest of the building was down to the studs. Our chef ran across the street to make food while we had a temporary bar. We also put up big tents.

Our staff gave a wonderful effort.

Island Hopper Returns

After the Island Hopper Songwriters Festival, the island returned to business as usual, which was slow. We had our food truck and Key Lime Bistro in Boca Grande open, but it took until late 2023 and early 2024 for Cantina Captiva, RC Otter's Island Eats and Sunshine Seafood Café & Wine

Bar to fully open.

I didn't expect that we would do a repeat performance for the songwriters festival in 2024, but we did.

Key Lime Bistro still wasn't done. This time I have my building permits for the electrical, plumbing and carpentry. It's a building with four walls and a roof right now. It'll be rebuilt and fully operational like it was before Hurricane Ian. The same with my Latte Da Coffee Shop.

My Captiva Island Inn had 10 Cottages torn down. It was painful to see, but they'll be completely rebuilt. Newly constructed units are scheduled to be completed three full years after Hurricane Ian.

Because of the loss of hotel room inventory and the lack of condominium rentals, none of the stores or restaurants are doing a booming business. It will take a few years to get there. We have to be patient and patience is hard when there is negative cash flow or break even. We try our best to get day trippers out to the island and that's when having a good marketing plan and team helps.

As my properties opened, Colleen and Earl Quenzel's marketing efforts helped make customers aware. We've worked together for 15 years and counting. While most customers make contact online, we did receive a phone call and a letter in the mail from two sweet, old-school ladies who don't use computers.

You just have to be adaptable. Yes, some people want to call or write. We are in a unique time when we have people like my parents who want to call and get their confirmation in the mail. They don't do email. So, in the day of everything computerized, we have to be careful not to lose some of our most loyal guests and customers.

Personally, it'll cost more than $10 million to rebuild. Some cottages were lifted right off their foundations.

Construction costs have skyrocketed. Insurance also has tripled. And once everything is up and running, we need to have affordable housing in an effort to counter the labor shortages. Some affordable housing is slated to start soon.

Why not sell? Why not walk away?

It's just not in my DNA.

Then, before our communities could catch our breaths, the islands took a few more hits.

We were once again put to the test. In September and October of 2024, when we were just months away from opening my final two restaurants two years after Hurricane Ian, we were hit with two hurricanes within a two-week span.

Hurricane Helene flooded the Inn and several of my restaurants and apartments. Then two weeks later, Hurricane Milton came with all its fury and totally flooded all of my restaurants, the Inn and even my Boca Grande restaurant.

Talk about a low blow! It just added insult to injury. I had just finished all of my new landscaping, sprinkler systems and lighting throughout. It was all washed away by a thick, slippery, stinky muck that covered everything in its path.

That's why storm surge is so devastating. It brings everything from the bottom of the Gulf and pushes it to the shore. It took the white sand from the beaches and pushed it all over.

The storms sent us back to dealing with insurance adjusters and deductibles. The damage was close to $200,000.00 per hurricane. Once again, all of the destroyed equipment and new furniture were put out on the street to be hauled away. It seemed like Groundhog Day. Life on our islands has plenty of benefits, but it also has its liabilities.

But when the going gets tough, I don't give up.

I dig down deep.

And I really want to see what our construction looks like completed. The plans are fantastic.

I have a new dream for our properties and want to use this opportunity to see what we can make of it. We want to have a blend of replanting palm trees and shrubbery, returning the Captiva Island look with the white and multi-colored picket fences; and maintaining that cottagey feel while having a resilience and being up to hurricane code that can preserve the properties for years to come.

Silver Anniversary

In 2024, I celebrated 25 years of business ownership on Captiva Island. Originally, I considered buying restaurants in The Bahamas and Costa Rica. However, certain labor laws and security issues kept me from going forward. I also considered buying a hotel and restaurant on Vanderbilt Beach in North Naples, but while the hotel made money, the restaurant lost money and I had no partners. I didn't even know what to charge for rent. If I planned on leasing it out, I clearly knew nothing about the financial aspects of running and owning a restaurant.

Instead, I realized that I needed to educate myself on the finer points of running a restaurant. In the hotel business, often restaurants are a part of the venture. So I rolled up my sleeves, researched schools and selected Cornell University's School of Hospitality Management. I saved and enrolled the following summer when my children were out of school.

Since I was a single mom, I asked my parents, sister and friends to care for my teenage children while I slept in dorms and studied.

I recognized I needed training for my own restaurant business.

With Vanderbilt Beach being developed and the Ritz-Carlton getting built, some people thought I missed out but I never doubted myself.

I have no regrets and I'm quite happy to have ended up on Captiva Island.

I always prayed that God would open or shut a door. Most people always ask for a door to be opened, but a closed door helps one avoid a path that may not have been best for them.

When the Captiva Island Inn became available, I bought that historical property, a bed-and-breakfast, which included seven cottages, a restaurant and offices at 11509 Andy Rosse Lane.

Pre-Emptive Moves

It didn't take me long to see a commercial threat to the island. Developers started to tear down a restaurant and cottages and turn that area into large homes. Then a few more businesses were torn down and large homes were being constructed.

I felt our village would disappear. I bought out my tenant in the restaurant that I turned into Key Lime Bistro in 2001.

Then I went to work and aligned with people who had the same ideas. When Helene and Marvin Gralnick, who started Chico's in 1983, came to me, they asked if they could turn an art gallery into a restaurant, even though their property was right next to mine.

I agreed.

In 2002, I bought Paradise Shopping Center, which included a real estate office, commercial shops and a small store with cottages in the back. One of the places we own used to be called Latte da Ice Cream and Deli, but we got rid of the deli. We fine-tuned that and turned it into a little mini-mart that sold books, suntan lotion and beer for those who need items at night. We then changed it to Latte da Coffee & Gifts. We followed that by buying two lots next to the inn and built the five-bedroom Celebration House and Celebration Center Business Plaza. About that time, I purchased RC Otter's Island Eats and Sunshine Seafood Café & Wine Bar. We were off and running.

Hurricane Charley came in August 2004 and halted development, but we began rebuilding after the eye of the storm went right through Captiva. It took about a year to fully recover. I anxiously awaited the South Seas to reopen, which was my major base of business.

Later I bought another restaurant and created Cantina Captiva as well as purchasing a four-bedroom home with a twin loft on the back bay. This gave me two large homes for weddings. The bride's family could stay in one and the groom's in the other. All of the cottages are perfect for the guests. If we had overflow, there were many choices.

Captiva Camaraderie

Fortunately, everyone I've done business with has become a friend. Maybe they liked selling to someone who also was drawn to Captiva's charms. There are no stoplights and no five-story homes, which helps preserve the five miles of beaches and the laid-back island community.

Many credit me to the point of calling it Sandy Rosse Lane. I giggled when I first heard that, but I wasn't really trying to get that name. I just wanted to keep the village intact.

The more the merrier, whether it's restaurants or shops.

I'm of the opinion that if there's one antique store people may not stop. But if there's two or three or five antique stores, they're more likely to stop.

We're friendly competitors. If I'm not interested in a property, I'll often suggest someone who may be.

Fellow restaurateurs and I work together. We share our staff. We share trash disposal areas. We brainstorm ideas. We do what we can to maintain the island's charm and see that older buildings don't get torn down.

I started a trolley service called S Car Go, but also helped on an ordinance where people could drive their golf carts on Captiva. It creates less traffic.

Before, restaurant owners had a parking lot and if you didn't eat there, you couldn't park there. We changed that. The main thing I want when people come here is that they have a good time.

We've been hosts for weddings, birthday parties, anniversaries, reunions, baptism parties, showers, rehearsal dinners, funerals, and so many life events.

Our chefs, managers and servers have gotten married and have children and grandchildren.

Customers and staff members have become like family. That's how a community is developed. That's very hard to turn your back on.

The AI story noted my "legacy of reliance" and "characteristic determination." And it added, "Captiva Island now stands as a beacon of hope and inspiration."

I'll take compliments like that any day – even if it's from a machine.

Entrepreneurial Mindset Q&A:

———————

Have you ever been emotionally connected to a town, city or state?

What have you done to keep that area thriving?

Do you feel it's important to have good relations with those you've done business with? Why?

Have you ever been in a situation where you've steered people to another business even if you don't benefit?

Have you ever been part of something bigger than yourself and you're serving the greater good?

CHAPTER 17

I Almost Bought An Island

"One day when standing at the pearly gates
and asked to describe myself and my
accomplishments I'll just smile proudly
and say: I did Useppa."

– Gar Beckstead, Useppa Island owner
from 1976 until his death in 2021

If you are curious, vigilant and open-minded, opportunities will come your way.

In fact, there will be more opportunities that come your way than you can accept. You have to say no to some.

It's important to know what's a good deal and what's a bad deal. And to know that, you have to go through those experiences. It's all part of the decision-making process.

In Kenny Rogers' song "The Gambler," he sang: You have to know when to hold 'em, know when to fold 'em.

One of those opportunities for me came with the chance to buy a piece of property: Useppa Island.

I've always been enchanted by Pine Island Sound, which

is encircled by Pine Island, Sanibel Island, Captiva Island, North Captiva Island and Cayo Costa Island. Pine Island – which includes Pineland, Matlacha, St. James City and Bokeelia – has a special attraction as well.

So when the chance came to buy Useppa Island just east of Cayo Costa Island and just north of the historic Pine Island Sound fishing shacks, I took a deep dive.

On so many levels, this seemed like a win-win-win-win-win situation.

My son Chauncey, who lives in Hawaii, would return home to help me manage the property.

Blake Gable, one of my potential investors, is the grandson of Barron Collier, who owned the island from 1911 to 1939.

I knew some of the residents because I had been a member of Useppa for at least 20 years. And many knew me because of the restaurants I owned on Captiva Island and in Boca Grande on Gasparilla Island.

And because of damage caused by hurricanes Irma and Ian, I had a pretty good idea of what needed to be done on Useppa Island. It had been affected by those two storms.

When taking on projects like these I always believed in collaboration. And that's not just with my investors, but in this case with those who live on the island as well.

I take pride in unifying people and groups. I like the synergy that goes on when we work for the greater good where everybody is enriched after the experience.

'Are You Here To Buy?'

In September 2024, my husband Tim and I took our boat Driller with friends to Useppa Island.

When we came down the dock, sister-in-law Dineen Post greeted us with the following question, "Are you here to buy

Family snapshot from Useppa Island of my son Chauncey and his family. From left to right: Chauncey, Nikki, Grace, Laila, me, Tristen and Ethan Brown.

the island? It's for sale and all these big people are here."

First, I didn't know Useppa Island was for sale.

Second, being a literal person, I wondered how tall these business people are. Are they NBA players? I hear they're as tall as 7-foot-4.

After sorting through my thoughts, I enjoyed the day on the island but when I returned home, I started researching.

Some things that I discovered, I already knew.

Useppa Island is a 100-acre bridgeless private island club. It is the perfect place to shut off from the outside world and relax. There's boating, fishing, kayaking, paddleboarding, bocce, tennis, croquet and more. There are approximately 135 homes, suites and cottages that take you back in time.

The New York Times once wrote, "Spend a day at Useppa and the outside world seems more than a boat ride away."

About 25 or 30 years ago, I was with a group from The Uncommon Friends Foundation, and we brought Anne Morrow Lindbergh, wife of decorated aviator Charles Lindbergh, and Silvia Earle, the first woman aquanaut to visit Useppa Island. What a memory! They loved the island and its rich history!

Gar Beckstead, who bought Useppa in 1976 and revived the resort from a jungle-infested, broken-down island, died at 82 on Feb. 16, 2021.

During the 45 years he owned it, Gar and wife Sanae told South Tampa Magazine they balanced what vegetation to cut back and what to let grow by hiring a horticulturist. While undertaking this endeavor, they discovered the island's past through archaeological digs while collaborating with the University of Florida. This led him to build the Barbara Sumwalt Museum, which shares Useppa's 10,000-year tale – from the Ice Age to the present.

The museum also includes the Useppa Historical Society.

Gar and Sanae also took the deteriorating 1,700-year-old structures and renovated them while building new homes and establishing strict deed restrictions to ensure new architecture was consistent with the old.

"Gar Beckstead was a brilliant, innovative man who was

devoted, head, heart, soul, to Useppa Island," Randy Wayne White told David Dorsey of The News-Press. White is a novelist and creator of the Doc Ford character and restaurants. "In the early 1980s, he rescued Useppa from ruin. He restored yet transformed the island into one of the most beautiful small treasures in the state.

"Gar was a kind, fun, tough and always supportive friend whose genius will last via his gifted family members and the magic that is Useppa Island."

So proud Gar was of what he created that he often shared this line, "One day when standing at the pearly gates and asked to describe myself and my accomplishments I'll just smile proudly and say: I did Useppa."

Useppa is full of history and mystery.

According to the island's historical society:

The Paleo-Indian people visited here in ca. 8000 BC.

The rising sea level made Useppa an island in ca. 4500 BC.

Barrier islands formed to create Pine Island Sound in ca. 4000-3000 BC.

The Tarpon Inn on Useppa Island.

Calahoosahatchee Indians began inhabiting the island from 500 BC to 500 AD, but from 1200-1700 AD, no occupation appeared to be present other than an occasional fishing camp.

Calusa Indians inhabited the island in the 1700s but they were believed to have been killed in war, enslaved or died of disease by 1750.

Yamassee and Uchise (Creek) people entered Florida from the north, bearing firearms.

Yamassee were bent on enslaving south Florida people for service in the Carolina colony; Uchise claimed some former Calusa territory.

Muspa Indians are reported to be living on Captiva, Sanibel and other nearby islands around the 1780s.

Around the same time, Jose Caldez of Cuba began using Useppa Island as the base for his seasonal fishing operations.

Useppa is where Seminoles – derived from the Spanish word cimarrones – were applied loosely to all Indian people in the Florida peninsula.

Now, island lore tells the story of notorious pirate Jose Gaspar imprisoning a Spanish princess named Joseffa. When she refused to return his advances, he killed her. Remorseful, he personally buried her on the beach. The island became known as "Joseffa's Island," which eventually evolved into Useppa.

"I don't believe any of that," Beckstead said, "but the middle name of my first-born daughter is Joseffa."

In 1863, Union soldiers camped on Useppa during the Civil War. Union sympathizers found refuge on the island under the protection of the Union army. Charlotte Harbor was blockaded to try to prevent beef shipments to the Confederacy. About 100 years later, The Central Intelligence Agency used Useppa for secret training of officers for a failed attack on Cuba to oust President Fidel Castro known as the Bay of Pigs Invasion.

Four privately owned bungalows housed 66 young Cuban exiles. The Collier Inn is where the CIA agents took up residence as its dining room was converted into the mess hall for the trainees.

Like Buying A City

Within a month of my visit, I shared my intentions through a letter of intent.

This process was like buying a city. However, with the CEOs and business owners, you're catering to upper-end clients.

My due diligence became a hefty-but-necessary expense, which included four different attorneys, engineering firms and surveyors, land planners, architects, accountants and a utility specialist while doing environmental studies and looking at solar components.

There were fun moments, like showing Blake Gable where his grandfather Barron Collier slept. He had been to the Collier Inn before, but not in the Barron Collier suite.

Barron Collier, who made much of his fortune by having advertising on New York's street cars in the 1890s, loved Florida so much he bought 1 million acres of land. He was a millionaire by age 26.

Tony Perrottet, writing for Smithsonian Magazine, penned, "By the Roaring 20s, Collier had built cottages, the golf course, his mansion and a lavish hotel where Prohibition could be ignored."

Visitors supposedly included the Vanderbilts, Rockefellers and Roosevelts; Thomas Edison and Henry Ford; and boxer Jack Dempsey, who partied with employees on a speck of land nearby dubbed Whoopee Island after the hit song "Making Whoopee."

Secretly, lovers Katharine Hepburn and Spencer Tracy made visits as did Shirley Temple, Perrottet added.

Problems Arise

When given an original list from the Homeowners Association Board, we had to redline a number of items in their 14-page proposal, which included no cutting down trees more than six inches. However, I thought we could work through those challenges.

After more than three months of due diligence, I met with homeowners at the Collier Inn on New Year's Eve 2023. I thought the meeting went great.

While I didn't want to add an assessment, I said the homeowners association dues needed to increase by about 40 percent because the fees didn't cover the true costs of maintenance to keep it to the standards that people expected. When Hurricane Ian hit in 2022, all costs rose by huge proportions even more than the normal inflation. No other fees would increase. We also planned on keeping the same real estate company.

I wanted to maintain the Useppa look and unpretentious charm while keeping the island's landscaping well-maintained. We knew how important this was to residents.

I was planning on building the additional homes and condos that were already allocated by the Lee County Building Department years ago. I planned on building a spa, improving one of the restaurants and putting in a large pool. Costly maintenance also needed to be done.

It was a large sum of money to invest and the only way to turn a profit was by having weddings and corporate retreats.

During this process, I prayed a lot. I didn't want my pride or long-time relationships to get in the way if this wasn't the right thing.

In fact, I told God that I needed the clearest sign possible.

When I did that, I had the most freeing and peaceful feeling in the world. Talk about empowerment! Talk about having a valuable relationship and resource, mixed with a loving, forgiving and accepting creator guiding me every step of the way.

"God," I said to myself. "I don't have any ultimate destination of what I should or shouldn't do. Whether I should or shouldn't buy this business. ... Whether I should take on this new responsibility or not. What is it you want for me?"

I'd also prayed: "God, I know I'm not worthy, but I know that you're worthy. Please forgive me of my sins and guide me. I want your will in my life. Let me know if you don't want me to do this because I'm going to move forward unless I get some roadblock along the way. So block me in a recognizable way."

The blocks couldn't have been much clearer.

There were five different associations with five different deed restrictions and there were different factions within the island. The promised streamlined proposal turned from a 14-page document to a 35-page document with more restrictions than the previous one.

After six months and two attempts at an agreement, we still weren't able to come to terms. I was on the last few days of due diligence when I received an unwelcoming letter from one of the homeowners associations. That was the sign I wanted. I didn't want to row upstream for the rest of my life.

The future of the island's ownership as of the writing of this book is uncertain, but I'm sure whatever happens, it will be in God's hands.

Entrepreneurial Mindset Q&A:

What is the biggest transaction you were involved in? What was it like going through that? What did you learn?

Did you feel you had done enough research beforehand?

Did you ask enough questions so you were comfortable with your decision?

Did you pray for your decision? What did your instincts tell you? Did you follow them?

Do you think you've had enough experiences in life to prepare you for your next transaction?

CHAPTER 18

Paying It Forward

"For it is in giving that we receive."

— St. Francis Assisi

Paris Kolar, my brother Tom's daughter, came into the world in 1989 at 1 pound, 9 ounces. Fortunately, doctors learned of a new medication and they decided to administer it.

She lived in Lee Memorial Hospital for the first six months of her life. At first, Tom and his wife, Melinda, couldn't even hold Paris. The best they could do was put their fingers on a cloth that touched the infant through a small hole.

Because Paris spent so much time in the incubator, doctors feared she would go blind. She didn't. She conquered every challenge. Back then, we didn't have a Children's Hospital or a Ronald McDonald House. Whatever issue she had, they transported her to Miami or other cities so she could see a specialist.

Paris went on to live a meaningful life full of joy and joined the family business with her brothers. She graduated from Canterbury School, then graduated from college.

But in those critical early days, the whole family felt so helpless. As kind of an appreciation for the wonderful work done by the staff at Lee Memorial Hospital, I got involved with helping to build Ronald McDonald House Charities of Southwest Florida. It was my way of saying thank you.

The mission of Ronald McDonald House is to create, find and support programs that directly improve the health and well-being of children and their families in Charlotte, Collier, Glades, Hendry and Lee counties.

Often, parents have to spend weeks at a time at Ronald McDonald House while their children are being treated at Golisano Children's Hospital of Southwest Florida, which was built in 2017. This is done at no cost. Sometimes, families also receive gift cards for food, gas or cell phones.

It's a well-known charity but many people believe the money

Our Southwest Florida Wine & Food Fest group received a tour of Golisano Children's Hospital before its opening. I was a fellow trustee with Jim Nathan, who was CEO and President at the time when we raised funds and helped build the hospital to support those in need.

comes only from McDonald's. It does not. McDonald's provided a seed grant to start and organizational support, but local owner-operators and community members needed to raise the money.

Karen Nathan, president of the Junior League and wife of former Lee Health CEO Jim Nathan, proposed the idea of raising funds to build a Ronald McDonald House, near The Children's Hospital of Southwest Florida. Spearheaded by the Frederic family, we raised enough funds in 1991 that the Ronald McDonald House became incorporated.

Five years later, in August 1996, the doors of the Ronald McDonald House opened to children and their families.

About 25 years after Ronald McDonald House opened, Jim Nathan asked me to co-chair a campaign that would fundraise so we could expand the facilities. Everyone knew the value of the charity and the money needed was raised that night.

Have you been involved with a charity? You won't believe how good it'll make you feel.

The Wealth With Purpose ministry, which seeks to help Christians become financially healthy so they can live generous lives, believes, "How we handle money is a reflection of our spiritual health. ... Generosity is a lifestyle. It is not something we do every now and then but daily. ... Generous people understand who the real owner is. We are stewards of God's resources. We are called to be generous with what he has blessed us with. You could say, 'We are to be generous to others like God has been generous to us.'"

Helping others through charitable endeavors by giving either your money or time to a cause, is highly rewarding and worthwhile.

Brian Rist learned the importance of giving back from his father.

"I've really been blessed in life, a very good life," he said. "I've been successful but what good is it if you don't share with others, share things you've learned.

"And you can give in many ways."

Besides giving Florida Gulf Coast University and the University of Massachusetts Lowell generous gifts, Brian has taught and mentored at those schools.

In 2024, he gave more than 100 scholarships to four different schools. I also was able to get him involved with the Southwest Florida Wine & Food Fest, which has raised more than $30 million since 2009.

"You give with the right reasons," he said. "You can't take it all with you. You also have a choice. Do you want to pay more in taxes or give to things you believe in?"

Scott Fischer also is a big believer in supporting youths

The secret to success with charities is that they work together. So much more of an impact can be made by the synergy of great organizations working in concert with one another, which is why I believe in the power of connectivity.

through scholarships and training. He's a big supporter of Junior Achievement, which believes in the boundless potential of young people.

"I'm a proponent of kids needing to work," he said. "It teaches them a level of respect and accountability. It changes kids when they work for somebody else."

Scott also has a family community outreach foundation, run by daughter Katie, which gives grants to local programs. And, he's overseeing a specialized company with four key employees. Part of the mission is providing powersports dealers, including Harley Davidson locations, digital leads for customers. The goals include providing better response times, quality showroom appointments and stronger sales opportunities for dealers.

"Three of them are leading different parts of it," he said. "I'm not really involved. We work on mutual training, coaching and digital academy. I don't have to be anywhere. I like what I'm doing."

Giving Lends Perspective

Even though life is hectic with a blended family and work, I still make time to lead or take part in a variety of charities, including the Southwest Florida Wine & Food Fest. We have raised over $30 million for Golisano Children's Hospital. As I said in a 2023 August/September issue of Florida Country Magazine, "I think sometimes we can get caught up in our businesses ... and so caught up in our own lives. That's why I'm more interested in acquiring food for soup kitchens. I also like being on boards of directors with my peers who are really wonderful. I learn a lot from them. I learn how to grow and how to ask a lot of questions.

And I think my heart will always be with children. Making a change in a child's life is special.

Over the years, I've been involved with dozens of charities and organizations throughout Southwest Florida. I've also willingly served on a wide variety of executive boards, which have included:

- Not-for-profit boards both locally and nationally
- University boards
- A magazine advisory board
- Bank boards
- Business organizations and associations
- Chamber of Commerce
- Governmental boards
- A church board

Many people have asked me why I get so involved.

Well, I really love Southwest Florida. There are a lot of giving people, whether they are full-time or part-time residents. I like to be surrounded by that spirit of wanting to help a community.

And I really enjoy working with colleagues from all businesses, from all backgrounds. I've learned so much from them, which has helped me grow.

Some people feel that what they're doing is almost selfish because they get back so much more than what they give. I feel blessed to be in the position to help. I'm honored to be valued and wanted as a board of director's member or trustee.

While Cape Coral has grown to Southwest Florida's largest city with approximately 240,000 residents, I have known this community from the start.

We knew the city's first physician, Dr. Robert Tate, and his nurses. We also know Gloria Raso Tate, a long-time Cape Coral council member who is Dr. Tate's daughter-in-law. Her sister Donna was the first girl born in Cape Coral.

We have been neighbors and friends since I was a young girl. It's a lifelong friendship and Gloria.

When he was young, my brother Tom quit breathing, and Dr. Tate recommended taking him from Cape Coral to Fort Myers where he needed to spend a few days in the hospital.

Paying it forward is much more than just raising funds to help a cause. Here I'm rolling up my sleeves with Habitat for Humanity on the raising of the wall for the house that Stilwell Enterprises sponsored.

I clearly remember the police guided my mom, my dad and Tommy through the roads until they arrived at Lee Memorial.

Sheriff Val Everly, a good friend, drove down the middle of the bridge, clearing traffic. His son Todd now runs the police academy.

The Rosens, the founders of Cape Coral, paid all of our medical expenses, even though Dad had just started with the company. You just don't forget those individuals in those emotional moments.

People helping people in their moment of crisis. That's why I pay it forward; and I do it with love and appreciation.

Entrepreneurial Mindset Q&A:

———————

What does your community mean to you?

Have you or a family member had a moment where community members helped during a time of crisis?

Are there any charities or organizations you've thought of joining?

If you are a member of a charity or organization, why do you do it?

CHAPTER 19

Losing Great Minds

———

"Sadly, I could say that the results
were not surprising."

— Dr. Robert Dicker, associate director
of child and adolescent psychiatry
for Northwell Health's Zucker
Hillside Hospital and Cohen Children's
Medical Center, on the increases
of suicides among young people

———

If it takes you eight hours to read this entire book, by the time you finish, the lives of five young people will end.

The sad thing is that due to depression, those young people ended their own lives. They died by suicide. It's the second-highest way we're losing these youths.

Mental health is a serious issue. While there are national concerns with teens and those in their 20s not finding jobs, there also are worries for those who don't have a work-life balance and become work-a-holics.

Dr. Alise Bartley, the founder and president of the Counseling for Community Wellness, said the two things she wants teens and college students to know are:

1. You are not alone. You shouldn't be ashamed to get help. Whether you have insurance or not, there are programs available.

2. Take the chance to talk to someone to improve your quality of life. It can be scary but solutions offered will improve your quality of life.

I was first introduced to Dr. Bartley through Children's Charities of Southwest Florida when I was the president of the organization. We funded $3 million for mental health through our Southwest Florida Wine & Food Fest proceeds. Part of the funding was going to Florida Gulf Coast University for a program that she set up to help students get counseling.

I was and am very impressed by her. She has now started her own counseling center.

"One of the best things of this generation is that they realize 'I need counseling,'" Dr. Bartley said. "They want to understand mental health and who they are. In addition, we've

Dr. Bartley has been a great advocate for providing better mental health services.

learned relapse from alcohol and drug use is part of recovery. The previous generation was about pulling yourself up by the bootstraps."

Dr. Bartley has more than 30 years of experience as a pioneer for multiple mental health treatment programs and is an activist for mental health services. She believes mental health is part of our soul, like breathing.

"We are improving outcomes one client at a time and CCW's retention rate is 80 percent," Bartley said. "The average is 30 to 50 percent. Having a face-to-face conversation and having a mentor, someone in a non-judgmental place, is important."

One of the few positive things that came out of the global pandemic, Dr. Bartley said, is that a great light shined on anxiety and depression while the stigma of mental health illness started to decrease. In a March 2022 report by the World Health Organization, in the first year of the COVID-19 pandemic, global prevalence of anxiety and depression increased by a massive 25 percent.

A Disturbing Trend

In a 2020 opinion piece in the New York Times by Richard Friedman, approximately 5,500 young adults die a year by suicide.

In another report by Health Day's Ernie Mundell, over 47,000 Americans between the ages of 10 and 19 lost their lives to suicide between 1999 and 2020, according to the peer-reviewed Journal of the American Medical Association. Research is showing the number is rising more among girls and women. The Kaiser Family Foundation's research shows suicide deaths are increasing fastest among younger people with many groups seeing increases of 30 percent or more from 2011 to 2021.

Then, combine that with Ohio State research finding adolescents and teenagers, ages 10 to 19, cumulatively losing nearly 200,000 years of life due to unintentional drug overdoses from 2015 to 2019, according to the report published in JAMA Pediatrics.

That's a lot of families devastated and a lot of potential doctors, nurses, entrepreneurs, teachers and other professionals whose lives ended far too soon.

Many of these deaths are tied to three areas – depression, mental health and social media. Not so ironically, those three areas often are interconnected.

Suffering Quietly

Do you know of anyone who has died by suicide?

I lost a very good friend who ended her life. She pulled away from our close friendship and I never understood why until I found out she was distraught and had made several attempts on her life. Everybody thought she was fine but she wasn't. While she battled silently, I still feel somehow I must have let her down.

Guilt often happens to those who see someone they know end their lives.

Dr. Bartley said some of the signs of depression are weight loss or weight gain, changes in sleeping patterns, feelings of sadness, hopelessness and worthlessness and lack of interest in pleasurable activities. She added suicidal people actually are more inclined to attempt ending their lives when they start feeling better. "When you are really, really depressed, you don't have the energy," she said.

Social media can be addictive. Likes on posts, funny videos or great messages give the brain hits of dopamine and serotonin that leads individuals to keep watching. But when there are negative posts or the likes on posts decrease or classmates have more responses, it can create a funk or depression.

"As social media became a primary area of teenage communication, that is when there was an increase in mood disorders, depression and suicide," said Dr. Robert Dicker, an associate director of child and adolescent psychiatry for Northwell Health's Zucker Hillside Hospital and Cohen Children's Medical Center.

Challenges Hit Close To Home

Personally, I've lived with family members who had mental health issues. The interactions have been nasty, scary, confrontational and terrifying. It put me in a highly uncomfortable position where I had to walk away.

When my son Erik started showing similar personality traits as his bi-polar father did 30 years earlier, I felt déjà vu. I had to say to Erik, "Do you realize you're doing the same things your father did when he was young? How did that make you feel?"

Erik, 40, like my son Chauncey is bright, talented and tough. Erik made it through four seasons of the reality TV series Deadliest Catch, which was shot on the Bering Sea near Alaska. In 2023, he persevered through crab season despite a broken hand so he's no wimp. It's high-intensity, high- energy work and it's what he thrives on.

However, Erik has a different battle. His is with drugs and his battle started when he was 24 and he's had legal issues going back to age 19. His choices of friends haven't been good. It's a cautionary tale for you to strongly consider who you hang out with.

Erik leaves treatment centers as a star pupil and model student who has convinced counselors that this is the time he'll continue being sober. Then he relapses. I understand that happens, like it does with cancer patients. Those in recovery can suffer setbacks.

However, I've literally had to bail him out time after time with fees and attorneys. He has crossed the line on what is acceptable behavior.

I've learned that Erik's true success will be when he no longer depends on me so I'm going to give him some tough love. He needs to be on his own and not rely on me as his fallback. I've cut him loose to live independently. A return to rehab may be good but that decision has to be 100 percent his, not mine.

I fear what could happen to him but I also remain confident he still can grow into the man I know he can be.

I will continue praying for him but my heart is broken.

I don't hide this because I understand these situations happen to many families.

Their addiction cannot be my addiction. It is so easy to be codependent and it really hurts both parties when that happens. It's not easy to separate yourself.

One of the things I've learned about myself is something I want to share with you: I am responsible for my happiness, and I owe it to myself to be happy. Happiness is a choice. You can be happy at any time, just choose to be!

If you are a family member for an addict, you can seek counseling as well. Al-Anon is a great program and there also is the National Alliance on Mental Illness (NAMI).

Please Seek Help

If the depression or mental-health issues are just too overwhelming, please seek help. Most college campuses have mental health counselors or licensed therapists to help. Some schools like Central Florida and South Florida often loan therapy dogs to students who may be stressed during a semester or before finals.

Even though the stigma with seeking help is disappearing, there is still a high percentage of students who don't see someone; and those are the people who are at a higher risk to hurt themselves.

While I strongly encourage you to reach out, also consider reaching out to God.

Pray or talk to God, scream or cry out if you need to. Sometimes the squeaky wheel gets the grease.

God wants you to know He loves you and He wants you to love Him. You're loved, just the way you are. He's waiting. Just go to Him.

I wish you well and all the best in pursuit of your dreams.

Get Immediate Help In A Crisis

There are so many ways to get help when you're feeling helpless and you're mentally, emotionally or physically drained. Taking action and talking to someone can make a world of difference.

You are not alone and help is out there for you. I promise you better days are ahead if you push through whatever you're dealing with at the moment.

I've listed below various ways you can seek help. I pray you will.

Call 911

If you or someone you know is in immediate danger, call 911 or go to the nearest emergency room.

988 Suicide & Crisis Lifeline

If you or someone you know is struggling or in crisis, help is available. Call or text 988 or chat 988lifeline.org. Calling 988 is a confidential, free crisis service that is available to everyone 24 hours a day, seven days a week. The 988 Lifeline connects people to the nearest crisis center in its national network. These centers provide crisis counseling and mental health referrals.

Crisis Text Line

Text "HELLO" to 741741 to receive immediate support from the Crisis Text Line, which is available 24 hours a day, seven days a week throughout the U.S. The Crisis Text Line serves anyone, in any type of crisis, connecting them with a crisis counselor who can provide support and information.

Veterans Crisis Line

Call 1-800-273-TALK (8255) and press 1 or text to 838255 to get instant support. The Veterans Crisis Line is a free, confidential resource that connects veterans 24 hours a day, seven days a week with a trained responder.

The service is available to all veterans, even if they are not registered with Veterans Affairs or enrolled in VA healthcare.

National Disaster Distress Helpline

Call or text 1-800-985-5990 to reach the National Disaster Distress Helpline, which provides immediate crisis counseling for people who are experiencing emotional distress related to any natural or human-caused disaster.

The helpline is free, multilingual, confidential and available 24 hours a day, seven days a week.

National Domestic Violence Hotline

1-800-799-7233
Text " LOVEIS" to 22522
TTY 1-800-787-3224

National Child Abuse Hotline

1-800-4-A-Child (1-800-422-4453)

Text 1-800-422-4453

National Sexual Assault Hotline

1-800-656-HOPE (4673)

Online Chat

Entrepreneurial Mindset Q&A:

Do you have any mental health challenges? Are you seeking help?

When something doesn't go right, can you bounce back after feeling down?

Do problems overwhelm you? Do you get depressed?

Why do you think teens and college students want to commit suicide?

Do you remember making a choice to be happy rather than being pulled into a negative situation?

What could colleges do to help youths with depression or mental health challenges?

Entrepreneurial Mindset Q&A:

As a business owner, are you prepared to lead your team through both professional and personal challenges?

You'll wear many hats as an entrepreneur, which sometimes could make you a counselor. Are you prepared to show compassion?

Being a source of positivity is often needed to run a business and motivate your staff. Are you prepared to be that shining light for your team?

PART 2: Notes

PART 2: Notes

Sandy's Entrepreneurial Checklist

I hope you enjoyed reading about the unpredictable journey of being an entrepreneur and how challenging yet rewarding the endeavor can be. There is a wonderful and exhilarating feeling you get from creating something that can help make lives better for others. It also doesn't hurt making a few bucks along the way.

Whether it's a book or a business, sometimes getting started can be the most challenging part. Below, I'm sharing a checklist that I hope will be helpful in beginning your journey. I've been told by fellow innovators that the steps outlined here have provided them with guidance and have saved them hours of work.

Good luck!

- Come up with a concept, vision and mission statement.

- Create a business plan.

- Develop a budget: Establish how you will finance your business over the next two to three years.

- Do you have the cash to start your business or do you need financing?

- Develop a marketing plan.

- Register for a fictitious name. Search to see if it is available.

- Search for your Corporate name to see if it is available.

- Apply for an Employer Identification Number (EIN) online, by fax or mail after selecting the name of your Corporation and DBA (doing business as).

- File for your corporation. Develop your corporate resolution. If you have business partners, come up with a partnership agreement that will steer you through conflicts and resolutions.

- Get a sales tax registration if you are selling services or products.

- Apply for a county occupational license, which is typically a local business tax.

- Apply for any license that is necessary based upon what type of business you plan on opening.

- Go to the bank and set up a checking account and order checks and deposit slips.

- Set up a Square account or some other easy way of accepting credit card payments directly.

- Set up Visa or Mastercard for a business account. Ask about protection for you with a business debit card vs. business credit card. I recommend a charge card for more protection.

- Establish accounting software to help you run your business. Quickbooks is used by many business owners, but there are other options out there.

- Set up files for receipts and expenses.

- Decide if your business will have employees or people working for you.

- If yes, choose a payroll service, staff leasing service or internally set it up. This decision needs to be made because you will need insurance for workers' compensation along with payroll tax set up.

- Get liability insurance and product liability insurance.

Acknowledgments

Because we don't choose our parents, I want to thank God for allowing me to be born as a child of Tom and Ellie Kolar. Being raised by them allowed me to be raised in a family that has shown me great love and trustworthy principles of commitment and hard work. They inspired me to never quit and showed me the true spirit of entrepreneurialism through their own examples of hard work. Their constant guidance has helped me know that they were always my sounding board and sometimes served as my backup plan, but never a crutch. They are my parents, friends and mentors.

I thank Jim and Ellie Newton for opening the doors to new friendships and relationships I never would have known without them. They taught me the value of listening and they were my mentors.

I am thankful to my Pastor, Jim Holbrook, who helped me on my spiritual journey that grew into leadership. He believed in me and my abilities. I served on committees in the church that women weren't typically allowed to be on or would have been chairman of. He encouraged me not to be afraid to speak out. It's only natural that he and Jim Newton were such good friends. He was my mentor.

I thank Paris Kolar, my niece who inspired me to become involved in not-for-profit charities. That little 1-pound, 9-ounce girl singlehandedly changed the direction of my life when she was a baby. Thinking that we would only have her for maybe a day, she lived until she was 35. She defied all odds and did it with a sweet and endearing demeanor. Her smile was infectious, yet she had great determination to excel. Even though there were disabilities, she graduated from high school and from college. She proved to herself that she could do anything, including going to motorcycle school with her older brother and passing the test that many men failed. Paris never rode a motorcycle after that. She simply wanted to do it. She didn't make excuses; she worked hard and made us all better people just by knowing her. I called her our angel and now she is watching over us.

I thank Don Stilwell for teaching me to hire good people, then hold them accountable and lead the leaders. Don't micromanage. He was my mentor.

I thank my husband, Tim Youngquist, for inspiring me by his example of how he runs his family business. He's been 50/50 partners with his brother for 56 years, and I am in awe of how they can divide and conquer with their individual talents and expertise. They recognized that they were greater together than apart. He's much tougher than I am, and it takes that firmness to run a good business and keep order. I'm constantly balancing the push-pull of running companies with many managers and staff. Having a sounding board and a partner who understands the pressures and challenges is priceless. Although we both were well-established in our individual businesses, he is a constant source of help to me, whether by loaning me equipment, advice or just a listening ear. Yet, in his toughness, true loyalty is created. His long-term commitment to relationships is to be admired.

I thank everyone who helped contribute to this book by sharing their story. It takes a team.

I thank Craig Handel, who helped me write this book and conduct the interviews with my friends. His true art is storytelling and writing. After interviewing me for an assigned article, a feature story about me, in Florida County Magazine, he encouraged me to write this book.

Finally, I want to extend a heartfelt thank you to Publisher Dave Kratzke, who was instrumental in our project. His wealth of experience and knowledge was a guiding light that helped us reach our goal.

About The Authors

Sandy Stilwell Youngquist

Sandy Stilwell Youngquist is CEO and owner of Stilwell Enterprises & Restaurant Group, which includes seven restaurants, an inn, shopping centers and a food truck. Her businesses are located throughout Southwest Florida, from Captiva and Gasparilla islands to Fort Myers.

She has been self-employed since she was 17 and has helped businesses and organizations alike, including helping to organize Gulf Coast Business Bank in Fort Myers, a de novo (new) community bank. She currently is on the Board of Directors. Prior to that, she was on the Board of Directors of Florida Shores Bank, which merged with Stonegate Bank and eventually sold to Centennial Bank.

The total number of organizations she is or has been associated with is staggering. She is a past president and a current trustee of Southwest Florida Children's Charities (SWFL Wine Fest), which proudly passed the $30 million mark in fundraising for Golisano Children's Hospital and other organizations, which helped purchase equipment and college scholarships for people entering pediatric health services.

She served on Resilient Lee, a group that delivered a comprehensive plan for hurricane resilience and rebuilding after Hurricane Ian. The plan was part of the $1.2 billion that Lee County received through the United States Housing and Urban Development. The plan fulfilled the required community input needed to receive the funds. The task force had several divisions, and she co-chaired the planning and capacity branch, which covered long-range planning and had its hand in every division.

Sandy is on the Executive Board of Directors of Hope Hospice of Lee County and is a member of the National Board of Chapters Health Care Affiliate Board of Directors, which is the largest in the Southeast United States for hospice care with the greatest focus in Florida. She is on the Board of Directors and Executive Board of The Horizon Foundation; a Board member of Junior Achievement of SWFL; a Board of Trustees and Executive Board of Habitat for Humanity; a Board of Trustees member of Pace Center for Girls National and she is on the Board of Trustees for Lee Health Foundation.

She serves on the Advisory Editorial Board of Gulfshore Life Magazine and the Advisory Board of FGCU Resort and Hospitality School-School of Business; The Captiva Community Panel; Healthy Lee, an Advisory Board for Lee Memorial Health Systems. Sandy is a member of the

International Women's Forum, an international organization of women CEOs. She also is a member of Junior League of Fort Myers and the Sanibel-Captiva Chamber of Commerce. One of her biggest sources of pride is co-chairing the expansion project of the Ronald McDonald House of SWFL. Working alongside Jim Nathan, retired CEO of Lee Health, she helped raise money and spearheaded construction of the Ronald McDonald House in Lee County. She served as Board President in 1999 and 2000. As a single mom, she sponsored a room at the House to set an example to her children that it's important to give back.

Her honors include:

- Gulfshore Business Lifetime Achievement Award

- The Community Foundation's Excellence in Nonprofit Performance Yearly Community Impact Award

- The State of Florida Senator's Pride Award

- Junior Achievement's Business Hall of Fame Laureate in 2017

- State of Florida Hotel & Restaurant Association Humanitarian of The Year Award

- Gulfshore Life Magazine's Men & Women of the Year Award

- Gulfshore Life Magazine's Philanthropist of the Year Award

- The Fort Myers Chamber of Commerce Apex Award (first woman recipient)

- Junior League's Community Service Award

- Sanibel-Captiva Chamber of Commerce's Citizen of
the Year

- Co-authored the character Education Curriculum for
the Uncommon Friends Foundation called "Lessons
Learned From The Uncommon Friends"

Sandy lives with her husband Tim in Fort Myers. She
enjoys boating, traveling and entertaining. With their
blended family of five children and 12 grandchildren, there
are plenty of opportunities to entertain.

Craig Handel

Craig Handel's entrepreneurial experiences began in the
small town of Deerfield, Wis. when he went door-to-door
selling pizzas and newspaper subscriptions.

The pizzas were for a high school fundraiser. The
newspaper subscriptions for The Deerfield Independent
allowed him to receive a free cassette recorder, which he
used for interviews.

Craig also coached Little League, delivered newspapers,
babysat local children, worked for the school lunch
program, was a camp counselor and wrote stories for the
Independent, nearby Cambridge News and Capital Times,
which helped him pay off his college loans six months after
he graduated.

Craig has written for newspapers in Wisconsin, Arizona,
California, Massachusetts and Florida since he started
writing in junior high.

Craig also has collaborated or is collaborating on six
books ranging from George Toma working the first 57 Super

Bowls as a groundskeeper; a boy born at 23 weeks; an Irish storyteller; optimizing mental performance in sports and life; building and developing nonprofits; and celebrating people's lives through legacy books.

He considers working on the baseball documentary Curveballs with John Biffar and David Van Sleet to be one of the most inspiring and rewarding experiences in his life. The men portrayed – who have lost limbs from either congenital defects or war injuries – offer their amazing perspectives on overcoming adversity and living a life of purpose and meaning.

An avid gardener and swimmer, Craig and his wife Isabel live with their puppy Ollie in St. Petersburg, Florida.

Thank You

Thank you so much for reading *Resilient Spirit*. It has been a pleasure to share my experiences with you. If you enjoyed this book, please consider leaving a review on the website where you bought the book.

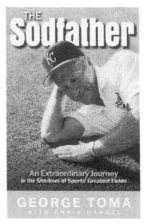